Elements of Theatre in *Dastangoi*

Elements of Theatre in *Dastangoi*

With special reference to Kashmir

Dr. Ayash Arif

AUTHORSPRESS

Worldwide Circulation through Authorspress Global Network
First Published in 2022
by
Authorspress
Q-2A Hauz Khas Enclave, New Delhi-110 016 (India)
Phone: (0) 9818049852
E-mail: authorspressgroup@gmail.com
Website: www.authorspressbooks.com

Elements of Theatre in Dastangoi

ISBN 978-93-5529-185-1

Printed in India at Thomson Press (India) Limited

Acknowledgement

I am thankful to the Ministry of Culture Govt of India and National School of Drama New Delhi for their support and guidance.

Dr. Ayash Aarif

Preface

Kashmir has been the birthplace of the greatest repertoire of stories that have percolated the folklore and folk literature of almost all Indian languages. Somadev's *Kathasaritasagara,* one of the all-time masterpieces of the world, comparable only to The Arabian Nights, *Panchatantarta* and Decameron was authored in Kashmir. There is no exaggeration in Hinton Knowles; the statement that "Kashmir as a field of Folk-lore literature is, perhaps, not surpassed in fertility by another country of the world..." (1887:xi).

A unique feature of the art of storytelling in Kashmiri, called " Dastangoi" is probably one of the oldest performance activities of the people of the region. Much of ordinary human discourse in the language includes stories in the shape of allusions (talmih) so that the discourse is made effective, interesting and convincing. A discourse aimed at convincing the listener that there is no end to tyranny and injustice, for instance, is supported by the legend "Proon Kafni Tchur Oas Nevyis Kafni Tchure Sindyio Khwata Rut, Laashyi Oas Ni Bya-Hurmati Karaan. (Old shroud thief was better than the new one as he did not desecrate the cadaver.) The immediate response of the listener is participation in the legend. There are hundreds of such allusions which are used in day-to-day social communication.

There is not anyone particular way of story-telling: stories have been told in many ways. Prior to modern times, music, drama, dance, and buffoonery was associated with story-telling. The art has, however, received a setback as a result of the onslaught of television and films, many professionals in the valley nevertheless pursue the art as their means of livelihood. Even a cursory study of this ancient art shows that storytelling is a performance art in its own right. The art of the storyteller can be enlivened, enhanced and supplemented by other forms of performing art, but the fundamental purpose of the anticipated study is to explore storytelling in Kashmiri as a unique art form that includes many elements of drama.

The subject matter of a story is always varied: myth, social satire, pure romance, frivolity, cuckoldry, bravery, cowardice and what not.

There are many stories that are serious about the unpredictability of human nature, unavoidable error and retribution; Tote Sinz Kath (A Parrot's Tale) is for instance one such story. Yet there are stories about the mystic recognition and soul's reunion with God like the story of *akinandun.* There is no dearth of such stories as are essentially meant to educate through entertainment. Whatever the subject matter, it is the dramatic presentation of the story that makes it an art. Since the art flourished in an oral culture, they are participatory in nature as the audience also becomes a part of the performance.

The book is a critical and analytic assessment of some of the most popular and permanent stories that have transcended the barriers of time and percolated down to the present generation through the art of story-telling. Some of the stories of this nature are:

1. Akinandun
2. Hiemal Neegyraay
3. Seny Kyisir
4. Toati sinz Kath
5. Laila Majnuun
6. Shireen Khusrav
7. Yousuf Zulaikha
8. Sheikh Sanaan
9. Shroud Thief
10. Shaal Geb Ti Haaki Tsar
11. The King married his mother

The book shall discuss in detail the dramatic element in the presentation of these tales by folk artists. Moreover, an attempt shall be made to explore the possibility of revival of this dying legacy and scope of innovations.

Contents

CHAPTER 1

Fundamentals of *Dastan* and its Presentation

The term '*Dastan*' in Kashmiri is borrowed from Persian and implies any long narrative in oral literature that relates the events of a remote age or some world of fantasy and imagination in accordance with the traditional stylistic formulae that are already known to the concerned audience. The artist involved in the act of narrating a *Dastan* might use his or her individual talent in making the events dramatic and interesting, but he/she cannot transgress the total framework of the art. Since *Dastan* is essentially a nicety of the oral literature, it thrives in all oral cultures and follows the rules and constraints of oral culture. Oral culture flourished in Kashmir, like many parts of India, up to the middle of the twentieth century when public education even at the literacy level did not exist. Since time immemorial, Kashmiris followed the agricultural and pastoral modes of living. They remained submerged in the oral culture that originated and sustained oral culture; reading and writing was a domain of the clergy and the genteel who had the prerogative of having leisure; reading and writing among the rural peasants and urban artisans and other working class was not even conceived of. It was believed that all the activities concerning reading and writing were meant for the selected few who were pre-ordained by divinity to do so. The competence had hardly any attraction for the toiling masses and they did not even think of it. Sir Walter Lawrence, whose magnum opus *The Valley of Kashmir* was published in 1895 from London, wrote about the state of literacy in Kashmir:

> ...the more affluent of the villagers prefer the mosque schools, or the system of private tuition, to the instruction given by the State, and it is a surprising fact that a large number of rural Muslims can read and write Persian with ease. The rural population does not at present want assistance from the State, and fathers have the old fashioned idea that homely morals are better than the scholarship and advanced thought which is born of the State schools. The State is also old-fashioned and

> recognizes that the supply of educated Pandits is already far greater than the demand, and that the manufacture at State expense of a number of hungry students, for whom there is no employment, would be likely to cause discontent. (p. 229)

Whatever the cause of the deplorable condition of education among the masses in Kashmir, our main emphasis here is on the fact that the society was deeply traditional and the feudal system did not support the idea of mass-education. There was a cynicism about the state-sponsored education and the government too did not desire that the working classes should pursue modern education as that might breed social disorder and ultimately protest. Thus among the population of 143,253 in Kashmir, only 233 Muslim students were on the rolls in 1891-92. (Lawrence 229) The figures are astounding for the present generation, but it was a bitter fact according to the Census of 1891. Our contention in the present context is to reveal that Kashmiri society was deeply conservative and preferred the traditional means of strengthening moral values; the concept of relating education to practical life was alien to the people. The state of education remained unaltered even up to the mid of the twentieth century when in the early years of the post-independence era the democratic government initiated the programme of public education as the most urgent programme to help the teeming millions, mostly Muslims, come out of the morass of ignorance and superstition by embracing modern education and relating it to their actual way of living. The programme of popularising the modern form of reading and writing and transforming society resulted in large-scale admission of the children of rural peasants and urban artisans to the public schools. Within a period of ten to fifteen years, the young men and women soon after achieving matriculation were recruited as school teachers who further popularised reading and writing as it could give them jobs in educational institutions. The curriculum was highly traditional as it mainly depended on literacy, memory and acquaintance with traditional memory-based subjects like history, geography, political science, education, literature, and classical sciences like botany, zoology, physics and chemistry. Consequently all the efforts of education yielded generations who could read, write and memorise. It did not influence any radical change in the beliefs, social relations, understanding of cosmic phenomenon, and change. It, in a sense aided the age-old culture and its mores. The only difference from the previous level of culture was that literacy became its integral part.

Oral culture, despite the state-sponsored programmes of universalisation of literacy, therefore, continued even up to the seventh decade of the last century and all the forms of education, entertainment and pastimes were essentially oral in nature. The society remained largely agrarian in nature which had a continuity of several millennia. The new society, though apparently modern and, to some extent prosperous, inherited the forms and media of ancient culture. In the absence of cinema, television, radio, and other electronic media, our society was happy with the legacy of the past like folk theatre, folk singing, folk tales, and roving entertainers. The orality was the hallmark of this culture even up to the sixth decade of the last century.

The oral culture possesses some unique characteristics that are universal in nature. It resists change and follows what has been handed over to the generations from the predecessors. It encourages the belief that whatever was the best in the world has already been thought of and realised in language; novelty was considered a transgression against the sacrosanct cultural mores, customs, and practices. The aesthetic corpus of a people, too, followed the same principle. In his book, *Technologies of the Self,* Foucault wrote:

> In traditional political life, oral culture was largely dominant and therefore rhetoric was important…by the Hellenistic age, writing prevailed and real dialectic passed to correspondence. Taking care of one's own self became linked to constant writing activity. The self is something to write about, a theme or object of writing activity…The new concern with self-involved *a new experience of self.* (28)

The culture before popularisation of writing did not have *a new experience of self*, but was determined by rhetoric and mnemonics. According to Walter Ong oral cultures have many characteristic features that are universal. He has discussed the issue of relation between orality and literacy in his much celebrated book *Orality and Literacy* which was published in 1982. The most distinguishing feature of oral culture is that speaking itself is an event, and every act of speaking is an action. People have greater respect for the words that a speech community inherits from the predecessors, and took great care in preserving the spoken literature as the dynasty's collective tradition or *kulaparampara.* No one could transgress the rules of oral literature and oral memory was preserved in mnemonic formulas. All forms of oral literature are therefore heavily rhythmic, full of patterns, repetitions, and musical.

According to Ong, the following features characterise oral culture:

(i) Oral culture is additive, rather than structurally programmed. It means that tales, legends, proverbs, riddles and fables are simply listed which could be endlessly extended. The components did not have any subordinate structure to form the structure of an experience that could be called the product of any one creative mind. It continues accumulating with the passage of time and belongs to all. It is largely folk. Thus a *Dastan* of the romance of *Laila wa Majnoon*, it can be retold freely without adhering to any particular hard and fast structure of any particular author, like Mahmood Gami. The narrator of the *Dastan* of the romance of Laila and Majnoon changes tone, tempo, the sequence of events, and language to adapt it to the situation in which participants are an integral part. He might even use many explanatory passages or make it more interesting by making references to similar tales, or innuendos and allusions. He is influenced by the audience that need full participation in the event of presentation.

(ii) All oral cultures are aggregative rather than analytic. It is full of ready-made expressions, stock phrases, stock responses and even clichés. The language is made more and more detached from the author by the use of hackneyed adjectives which tend to get adhered to the words. This feature is essential for oral literature to help the folks to recall it and in more or less unaltered form. The *Dastan* of *Hiymaal Naegyraay* for instance is recounted always in its traditional form. The narrator cannot introduce his personal import to the elements of fiction.

(iii) All folk forms of oral literature are copious and full of redundancy. For memorability, and playfulness of a Dastan the narrator uses open ended expressions in accordance with the mood. For instance, if a lovelorn character complains of his sufferings, he goes on adding more and more outpourings of grief and pain so that he fills in the time at his disposal. We can add and slough off many passages without making any significant difference to the story or song.

(iv) All forms of oral literature, including Dastans, are conservative and traditionalist. It solely depends on the memory of the elders of a clan or society who narrate it verbatim. It has no reference to any particular moment of milieu. It is free from time and space. The narrator does not, and cannot, add the issues and problems of his own time to the *Dastans* which he has bequeathed from his predecessors.

(v) The forms of oral literature are used in every age not merely as a means of storing folk knowledge, but also for intellectual debate. The user of proverbs, riddles, fables and tales aims at countering the opposite's point of view or to undo some common perception. The *Dastan* of *Akanandun*, for instance, is retold repeatedly only to ascertain the idea that the destinies of human beings are preordained and also to support the idea of ancient belief that real annihilation in the material world leads to affirmation. Similarly, the segments of an oral society keep using folk forms of literature to support their preconceived notions inherited from ancestry.

(vi) Folk literature is participatory rather than objectively distanced. This idea of Ong means that the audience, too, participate in the act of performance. He already knows the subject as well as the matrix of the performance, his entertainment is complete when he himself gets involved in its presentation. Oral societies are by and large, what Ong calls 'homeostatic'; that is they live in the present. The story of the oral performance does not belong to any bygone age but to all times. The audiences identify themselves with the characters involved in the *Dastans*; the past is altered to suit the needs of the present. A bard of a tale, like Hatim Tilwoony, keeps the meter regular, and uses the same formulas and themes, but stitches them together in a different manner every time in accordance with the nature of the listeners, their mood, their age, social status and biases. The successful narrator is one who is sharp enough to understand his audience; he performs in the participatory present, and, as such, the oral performance is dynamic.

(vii) Oral literature is occasioned by the lived present world. It does not deal in abstract ideas, categorical definitions, introspection and the meditative reflection that results in

> analysis of the particular self. It is essentially situated in a social context and represents the pragmatic lived world. It does not allow establishing autonomous, context-free discourse. It is best when it is actually lived through with the help of an expert narrator. All words and verbal expressions, unlike written literature, depend on actual sayings through speech mechanisms. Even the accent, dialectal variations, speech rhythm, word-play, rhyme, intonation and idiosyncratic variations of tone become functional.

The seven salient features of oral literature, discussed by Walter Ong help us understand the nature of the art of *Dastan goi* that flourished in a culture that preceded the popularisation of modern education through printed books. It is an art that is fundamentally in the domain of folklore. Before we analyse various elements of *Dastan goi,* it is important that we understand the nature of folklore.

Folklore, like culture, is an ambiguous term defined variously by various folklorists. After assessing its various definitions we understand that it is a corpus of collective concepts about man and his relations with the external world and man's communal practices that have currency in order to give expression to those concepts. In folklore the individuality of an individual ceases to exist as it dissipates into the amorphous individuality of the community. In the words of the greatest theoretician of folklore, namely James G. Frazer, folklore is "collective actions of the multitude." (1919: vol.ii. 211)

The term folklore was first used in the eighteenth century when a famous German philosopher John Gottfried von Herder (1744-1803) who coined three terms in the German language: *volkssele* (=folk soul), *volkglaube* (=folk belief) and *volkslied* (folk song) for the much celebrated anthology of German folk songs. The English term folklore was coined in 1846 by Thomas, and it meant traditional customs, tales, sayings, riddles, and art forms preserved among a community in a certain geographical terrain.

The term was immediately popular as it was in consonance with the romanticism and nationalism of the times and eventually several societies of folklore were established throughout Europe and America. From its very beginning the study was guided by romantic nostalgia and was aimed at the exploration of the past and finding the unique characteristics of various communities that constituted their national identity. The romanticism of the nineteenth century in

Europe had an irresistible fascination for the rustic, natural, and pastoral cultures and as such folklore from its very inception was centred in the agrarian cultures and pastoral harmony between man and his surroundings. Underlying the studies was the yearning of the urban middle class to find means to remove the alienation between man and nature and was aimed at revival of the past so that the alienation caused by the progress in material culture was defeated and that mankind could live in complete euphoric harmony with the forces of nature. The penchant for the primitive, rustic, savage, illiterate, simple among the intellectuals of the city was essentially ethnocentric and, as such, gave strength to the nationalistic aspirations of various ethnic groups and communities that fought for the assertion of their nationalistic identity and independence.

In its initial stage of development folklore was not an independent sphere of inquiry, but was subservient to overall politics of a society living in a particular bourgeois socio-economic structure, mainly in the cities. It was known by the existence of its binary opposites, that is the urban, elite, commercial, genteel, educated and sophisticated. It more or less meant the nomadic, vulgar, illiterate, peasant, and the pastoral section of the society. It belonged to the section of society that was called *vulgas* in *populo* that stood in contrast with the sophisticated and civilised section of the same society. The people living in the cities with a commercialised way of life and having all their value systems determined by the capital, used to use the term in its pejorative sense so that they could define themselves as an in-group; the folks to them were an out-group. Any interest in folklore was, therefore, guided by class-ego and romantic escapades, and, in certain cases, romantic licenses. However, the romantic poets and fiction writers created a romantic halo around the concept by associating the notions of the sacredness, innocence, simplicity and immaculate nature with it. We have, for instance, several highly charged sentimental poems of Wordsworth, Keats, Shelley and others and several novels like the world-famous masterpiece *Wuthering Heights* of Emily Bronte in which we get the illusion of the folk glamorised. We could not have the concept of the folk in primitive societies as city life pivoted on business did not exist.

Scholars' enthusiasm to collect information about the folks was primarily motivated by the urban sense of superiority as if they wanted to show what the barbarian, and savage life was that stood in sharp contrast to the civilised way of life. Here is Andrew Langue's opinion about the folklore.

> There is a science, Archaeology, which collects and compares the material relics of older races, the axes and arrow-heads. There is a form of study, folklore, which collects and compares the similar immaterial relics of older races, the surviving superstitions and stories, the ideas which are in our times but not of it. Properly speaking, folklore is only concerned with the legends, customs, beliefs, of the folk, of the people, of the classes which have least been altered by education, which have shared least in progress. But the student of folklore soon finds that these un-progressive classes retain many of the beliefs and ways of savage… The student of folklore is thus led to examine the usages, myths, and ideas of savages, which are still retained, in rude enough shape, by the European peasantry. (1884:11)

This folk-as-peasant definition of folklore remained the most accepted definition up to the twentieth century. Most of the anthologists of folklore were guided by their sentimental zeal to salvage and preserve folklore as it was, in their opinion, to die soon because all the peasants would sooner or later get urbanised.

There was no concept of urban folklore. It was also believed that folklore would ultimately vanish under the onslaught of modern means of entertainment like radio, television, films and other computerised methods of delight. There would also be a sort of mixing together of all cultural groups as the modern ways of living in terms of food, dress, housing, games, and other means of recreation are every day being homogeneously accepted by all peoples of the world irrespective of their traditional past.

Folklore therefore was initially defined in terms of certain binary opposites to the characteristics of urban elite culture.

The differences emerged particularly after the advent of the printing press when literacy became a right of the general public, particularly the urban middle class.

Some of these binary opposites could be listed as below:

URBAN	**RURAL**
Written	Oral
Literate	Illiterate
Additive	Subordinative
Analytic	Aggregative
Genteel	Rustic
Individual	Collective
Objectively Distanced	Participatory
Upper Stratum	Lower stratum

Famous American folklorist Newel proposed a wider and more accommodative definition of folklore. In his words, folklore is:

> ...information and beliefs handed down from generation to generation without the use of writing. (1890: 23)

Folklore thus became an umbrella term for a wide range of oral texts like fables, tales, beliefs, esoteric practices, magical chants, riddles, parables, proverbs, and other genres of communal mnemonics. Folklorists, therefore, extended their quest for all these relics of the past as if they wanted to preserve the dying oral culture of the aborigines, nomadic tribes, insulated ethnic groups, immigrant groups, and the agrarian populace. They undertook the task as a mission as they considered it as a part of their religious duty. In fact all the Christian missionaries devoted their lives for collecting and recording the fast dying oral culture as they knew that it would facilitate their propagation. To them the forms of folklore and folk literature could be used as vehicles for their message because the general populace understood all wisdom and knowledge through folklore.

The study of folklore also received an impetus when the Marxists, much like the Christian missionaries, realised that the most effective way to reach the common masses was to use their traditional culture as a means of disseminating the revolutionary message. In order to motivate peasants and the proletariat to cause a revolutionary change in society, it was necessary to use the language of the masses and their ways of expression. The Marxist ideologues not only revitalised the pre-capitalist era myths and romances, but also encouraged creation of new myths in support of various people oriented political precepts. A large number of poets and fiction writers used old myths and legends as a means of communication and at the same time created special conditions of the languages that facilitated the generative potential of the language of the masses to produce more myths. During the Marxist rule in the erstwhile USSR, writers, artists, folklorists and opera artists worked day and night to rejuvenate folk literature, but quite selectively and combined it with modern art. The basic aim was to motivate people to play various social roles and inspire them to contribute to the development of society in whatever way they could. Each folk tale and song was carefully recorded so that instead of strengthening superstition they contributed to the establishment of a rationalistic society in which man lived in harmony with the elemental forces of nature.

In fact every language has its potential that needs to be harnessed for a purpose. All languages in the agrarian societies flourished in the mythopoetic conditions that characterised the primitive societies, but after the advent of capitalism, languages gradually lost this energy because the languages were used for commercial purposes and objective discourses. Since a myth is not in itself an object but a means of signification, creative writers can create an appropriate ambience that can energise the inherent myth making power of the languages. In Roland Barthes' words "Myth is a Type of Speech". He wrote:

> Of course, it is not any type: language needs special conditions in order to become myth: we shall see them in a minute. But what must be firmly established at the start is that myth is a system of communication that is a message. This allows one to perceive that myth cannot possibly be an object, a concept, or an idea; it is a mode of signification, a form. (1957: 32)

Barthes asserts that myth is a type of speech and a semiological system that can be employed for encoding a special message and as a means of communication. Marxist writers knew this and used it for political propaganda. The result of this utilitarian approach to myth augmented myth studies as an end in itself as well as a means of signification in the post-mythic era. The study of myth immediately got associated with other disciplines of knowledge like literary criticism, anthropology, culture, linguistics and psychology.

The modern concept of folklore is, therefore, altogether different from that of the nineteenth century anthropologists and folklorists. It is now believed that folk does not necessarily mean peasants, shepherds, nomads and immigrant groups, but people in general. Alan Dundes wrote:

> ...the term folk can refer to any group of people whatsoever who share at least one common factor. It does not really matter – common language, or common religion – but what is important is that a group formed for whatever reason will have some traditions which it calls its own. ...The group could be lumberjacks, rail roadmen, or coal miners, or Catholics, Protestants, or Jews. The members of a country, a state, or region, a city or a village, a household or family, are all members of groups, and thus there is national, regional, village and family folklore. (1975: 7)

In view of this changed notion of the word "folk" it is possible to catalogue many other groups under the category folk: students of a college or a school in a particular locality, the male school teachers and the female school teachers, University teachers, research scholars, senior students and the junior students, actors, film producers, doctors and the para-medical staff, and so on and so forth; the catalogue could be extended in all possible ways. The fact is that any group, according to Desmond Morris of *The Human Zoo*, is recognisable as a cultural entity in contrast to some outer group. The combative relation between a group and the outer group creates disparate cultures and subcultures and each culture chants, etc., collectively called the folklore of the group.

Since the groups and outer groups are never fixed and big or small is identifiable in terms of its slang, phatic utterances, argot, legends, anecdotes, nonsensical rhymes, continue to change with the changing socio-economic situation, there are infinite possibilities of emerging of new groups, and as such, there is no end to the emergence of ever-new folk-lore that becomes the defining characteristic of the cultural identity of that group. Roman Jackobson is right in saying that all the folklore of the human race is a universal language and each human being is endowed with the intrinsic competence or *la langue* (Ferdinand de Saussure's term) for creating fresh lore; every performance of that natural competence is the *la parole* (Ferdinand de Saussure's term) as that of a natural human language. The anthropological importance of folklore in the making of man as homo sapience is tremendous as it is the substratum of all his desires, dreams, illusions, and all his strife to transcend the boundaries of the finite existence and attain infinity. "Who are the folk?" Alan Dundes posed the question and proposed a pat reply to the question: "Among others, we are!" (1975:12)

In view of the arguments given above, folklore can be defined as a the sum total of all the collective linguistic parole, through a certain duration of time, of a group determined by geographical position, common vocational interests, temporal contingency, salary, economic status, or uniform. The lore of the particular folk is conserved and handed over from generation to generation orally with or without recording. Even in the modern technological age folklore originates and gets accumulated; even the high tech audio-visual means play a role in giving birth to folklore through television ads and popular rhymes. All the pop rhymes of films and albums are consigned to memory of the populace and are repeated and even parodied by folks with or without any reason.

All folklore springs from man's individual subconscious which cannot be isolated from the collective consciousness. In his works like the *Interpretation of Dreams*, *Totem and Taboos*, and *Jokes and Their Relation to the Unconscious*, Freud through his empirical studies asserts that the whole phantasmagoria of the unconscious springs from the irrational part of the mind, called the Id, and gets expressed in the form of dreams, paranoia, poetic imagination, myths, fantasy, fancy, superstition, and archetypes. In the Id the whole pre-linguistic substance remains amorphously mixed together that determines the unconscious behaviour of individuals.

Carl Jung, however, sought the basis of the unconscious in the collective archetypes of the human race. In conformity with Jung's collective unconscious, Joseph Ryson proposed a broad definition of folklore:

> Folklore can be defined as the collective objectification of basic emotions, such as awe, fear, hatred, reverence, and desire on the part of the social group. (1952:10)

An essential characteristic of folklore is the anonymity of its authors. Every folklore event, whether story-telling, performance of a magical chant, a ritual, or a folk-performance, happens in a group situation. The teller or the performer has an organic relation with his audience. The latter knows not only the performer, but the contents and the context of the folklore event and thus the performer and the audience constitute a certain reference group. Dan Ben-Amos writes:

> … they speak the same language, share similar values, beliefs, and background knowledge, have the same system of codes and signs for social interaction. In other words, for a folklore communication to exist as such, the participants in the small group situation have to belong to the same reference group, one composed of people of the same age or of the same professional, local, religious, or ethnic affiliation.[24]

In this framework the teller of a tale, performer of a folk-drama, or ritual and the audience "are all related to each other as components of a single continuum, which is the communicative event." (1982:14)

The forms of folklore are variegated: tales, fables, parables, legends, proverbs, riddles, beliefs, songs, performing arts, group dances, musical performances, customs, and rituals. All these forms are transmitted in a social group or linguistic community from one generation to another as a sacred legacy. But in spite of people's familiarity with the text, texture and context of every event, it sounds always new to the audience. A child will never recite a folk rhyme unless he or she is convinced that the rhyme is a fresh individual invented creation of the child. The simplicity of the child's imagination is common to all forms of folklore.

Every form of folklore belongs to one of the three categories: a kind of art, a body of knowledge or a mode of thought. It may, however, encompass all the three domains. Thus no form of folklore can be divorced from the mode of a community living in an ecological situation. It is a people's response to the geo-physical conditions that always circumscribes them.

Although all forms of folklore originate from the subconscious mind that has no connection with the ambient objective world, it, being expressed in the form of language or social behaviour, gets impregnated with references to the objective social reality which a linguistic community passes through. Up to the end of the nineteenth century, folklore was believed to be representative of the past. A historical approach to folklore treats it as a source of knowledge for the anthropological interests. It is primarily based on Freud's notion of folklore, like religion, as a projective system derived from infantile life and for a community, living in a particular location, the infantile life is its primitive phase of culture. Thus concepts of space, time, weight, number, colours, sizes, distance, direction, limits, and such similar logical and semantic categories vary from culture to culture and folklore provides us the means of studying these concepts from within the culture. It is according to the anthropological theory, an expression of man's struggle for survival that man is seen in direct relation with the elemental forces of nature, animate as well inanimate. All folktales, folk songs, riddles, folkdances, and folk games are derivatives of earlier myths and rituals that the primitive man used to make his life easier.

The tales, parables, proverbs, riddles and other forms of oral folklore function as vehicles to carry the experiential legacy of a community from one generation to another. Many of the parables get crystallised in the form of pithy sayings that are called proverbs. Allen Dundee wrote:

> Like other forms of folklore, proverbs may serve as temporal vehicles for personal communication. A parent may well use a proverb to direct a child's action or thought, but by using a proverb, the parental imperative is externalised and removed somewhat from the individual parent. The guilt and responsibility for directing the child is projected on to the anonymous past, the anonymous folk. (1975:32)

It is believed that the genius, wit and spirit of a nation are discovered in its forms of folklore.

It may be summed up here that folklore is real people's speech that gives continuity to a community in teaching the successive generations of that community the experience that could not be stated in a discursive way or in terms of sermons, but delightfully through imaginary characters and events.

Folklore, though universal in import and significance, reflects the changing patterns of life in total accord with the ecological, geographical situation and the corresponding mode of life of the people. It is in the texture, text and context that a folklorist can find the reflections of society. Every form of folklore, whether verbal or non-verbal, has to be studied in relation to the time of its creation even if it is accepted and preserved from its context. A proverb or a riddle, for instance is timeless in terms of its semantic significance and utility in communicating wisdom, wit or humour, but its text, texture and context cannot be understood unless we know the material reality of the social context in which it originated. A structural study of any piece of folklore is possible only if we study its historical background. Folklore is definitely a reflection of man's concept of the structural relation of the individuals of a society. No character or event in folklore is in isolation, but projected as a part of the complex inter-relationship of various sections of society living together in a particular common mode of living. The concept of individual characters owes it origin to the industrialised society of which the short story, the novella and the novel are the representative genres. All forms of fiction in folk literature belong to the pre-industrial society, chiefly the nomadic, pastoral and agrarian. All characters are type characters and all events are stereotyped in folk literature. Some stock characters in the *Dastans* reveal their universal import; here are some of these characters:

King

In the social hierarchy, the king is the supreme authority in all *Dastans* The King of the country is to be respected and obeyed even if he is a blockhead, for he is the *zul-I Ilahi*, God's vicegerent. However, in most of the folk tales of Central Asia and Kashmir kings are shown as stupid, impetuous, and irascible people. They depend totally on their Vazir (Chief Minister) for counsel. The kings in folklore are idlers, cowards, and remained engrossed in frivolous entertainments like the flat jokes of the chief fools in their courts. The king has many wives and one of them is his favourite queen and thus the soul inheritor of his estate. The king when convinced about the goodness of a person is all out to reward him or her.

Queen

The queens in folk tales are exceptionally pretty but given to all kinds of deceit and lasciviousness. The queen in the Central Asian and Kashmiri folk tales remains confined to the palace where she enjoys illicit relations with their attendants. The queen is invariably clever and gives good counsel to the king whenever he is in a crises.

Vazir

The Vazir or the Chief Minister is the alter ego of the king for he is the decision-maker and thinks for the king. In certain tales the Vazir is shown as jealous of the king and conspiring to usurp the king's position and power. But in most of the tales, the Vazir solves complex problems and helps the king to rule the country.

Here is a beautiful folk tale from Kashmir in which the King and the Vazir are shown in agreement on a noble cause. The Vazir makes the king understand the advantages of forestation and also realise his power and position.

Wise Peasant

Long long ago, there lived a king who was kind, and pious and was keen to learn from others. He wished that all his subjects were kind, sagacious and pious. In order to learn from others and encourage goodness among his subjects he used to wander in his country in disguise and enquire about the well-being of his people.

One day accompanied by his Vazir, while on an errand, he saw a feeble old man planting fruit trees on a sunny plateau. The lonely old man was heavily perspiring and yet engaged in his wok. The king was amazed to see his fortitude. He went near him and asked him politely," Hello dear old man, do you know you are very old ?"

"Yes, I am in my eighties." Without looking at the King he smiled and said.

"And do you know you are planting fruit trees that will take a very long time to grow and bear fruit?"

"Yes, I know that. But what then?" The old man stopped and asked the king.

"You will have died by then, to be frank."

"Yes I know. Do you see those yonder trees laden with fruit?"

The King saw the full-grown fruit trees standing at some distance.

"These are the trees that were planted by my grandfather and his father. And the fruit of the trees is for me. So I plant new trees for the sons and daughters of tomorrow."

The king was pleased to hear the old man's reply. He ordered his Vazir to give him a pouch full of gold coins.

"Hah, hah, hah !" the old man laughed loudly while accepting the reward.

"Why do you laugh?" The King asked the old peasant.

"Don't you see the seedlings that I am planting have started giving me their fruit?" pat came the peasant's answer.

The King, amazed by the peasant's prudent reply, ordered his Vazir to give him another pouch of gold coins.

The Vazir obeyed and gave him a second pouch of gold coins.

The peasant laughed again and said, "Trees come to fruition but once in a year, you see, the seedling that I sow gave me fruit twice when I have hardly planted them."

The King was all the more amazed by the old peasant's wit and ordered his Vazir to give him a third pouch of gold coins.

"God Save the King! I cannot obey the order," said the Vazir.

"What !", enraged by the Vazir's impudence, the King shouted.

"Your Majesty, the old peasant is very prudent and knows the time is yet to come. Let us leave him to his condition and save the treasury."

The King reflected for a while and rode away to another village.

The tale thus communicates through the Vazir and the wise peasant the centuries old folk tradition of the importance of environmental conservation. The Vazir in the tale also stands for sagacity and prudence in governance when he advises the king not to be carried away by sentiments while appreciating the goodness among people so that the people's wealth is not wasted in gratifying the egoistic considerations of rewarding people. The masses have their own wisdom that keep the world running according to their own naïve sense of doing good without any motive of getting appreciation.

Pir

Kashmir like other countries of the whole of Central Asia, abounds in Pirs that form a social sect. All over the territory there are shrines in the names of various Pirs and people have veneration for all these shrines, known as *Ziarats, Aastaans and Khanqahas.* Annual fetes are held at these shrines in which people show great enthusiasm and jubilation. But throughout Central Asian countries, it is commonly said that the real Pirs existed in the past and the Pirs of the present are corrupt and only impostors. Hinton Knowles wrote in his book *Kashmiri Folk Tales*:

These Pirs (spiritual guides) are wretched lot of fellows—ignorant, negligent, sensual, selfish. They are supported by the inhabitants of their different villages, and are thought to be possessed of sanctity and spiritual powers of pleading before God. This conviction, of course, has to be supported, encouraged and contrived at; otherwise the poor, ignorant, superstitious villagers would withdraw their support.(1893:135)

Here is a story about a Pir, titled: *The Pir of Phattapur*

The Pir of Phattapur

A Pir once visited a certain village of which he was the spiritual guide to see his disciples. On his arrival they all gathered round to welcome him, and all promised to send him food. However when evening had come, each one, hoping that some others would look after the Pir, did not bother. The consequence was the Pir got nothing, and was obliged to fast. For his own credit's sake he could not go out and beg.During the night a great wind sprang up and constantly burst open the door of the mosque where he was staying. Each time he thought that somebody had come, and rose to receive them; but alas ! it was only the wind. On the following morning his disciples gathered round him and asked whether he had been comfortable, when he reproached them for their negligence; whereupon the people began to abuse one another for not bringing some food for the Pir. "*Chanih pirah korih nikah ! Chaani piri korih huni niwan ! chaani pirh korih rani* !" said they, which words mean, "May your pir's daughter be married! May your pir's daughter be carried off by a dog ! May your pir's daughter (have lots of) husbands !" Of course all the abuse fell on the head of the pir who was so disgusted with them that he took up his wrap and went.

The Pir is believed to save his disciples from the evil eye, bad men, disaster, cure illness, and bring them prosperity. The Pir is believed to be omniscient and by virtue of his command over magical chants can accomplish even the impossible. He can make a barren woman give birth to a child, he can determine the sex of the conceived baby or he can recover lost property without any investigation.

Faqir

Like the pirs, the faqirs are also castigated for their deceitful ways in swindling innocent folks. They wander from village to village and pretend to be the saviours of people. The faqirs are venerated and sometimes feared for their having the power of bringing good fortune or casting spells on people and are therefore provided alms so that they are happy. As in Central Asia, faqirs are also believed to utter their blessings or curses in cryptic words that are not easy to decipher. Here is a story about a faqir that has many parallels in the Central Asian folk literature.

The Prayerful Faqir

Once upon a time there lived a poor man with his two children, a son and a daughter. He was reduced to circumstances that he had not food or clothing for them, and was obliged to beg alms from house to house in almost a nude condition. One day, in the course of their peregrinations in quest for food, they met a holy and virtuous faqir, concerning whom it was reported that he never failed to obtain direct answers to his prayers. On seeing this holy man they made their salams, and begged him to pray for the relief of their poverty. The faqir directed them to a certain place, saying that if they entered that place one by one and heartily offer up their prayers it should be granted them. "But be very careful," he added, "and only ask for one thing." Then the faqir departed.

The daughter was the first of the trio to enter. She lifted up her voice and prayed for beauty, and her request was vouchsafed. She came forth to her father and brother a blooming, beautiful girl, with whom the king, who at that time happened to be passing by was thoroughly fascinated. His Majesty stopped, at once offered marriage and was accepted. The quickly-found lovers rode off together.

But the father did not quite agree to this sudden separation from the daughter, and, besides this, he was exasperated by her remaining so long within the praying place. Accordingly, full of angry thoughts, he entered the place, and asked most earnestly that the Mighty One would afflict his disobedient, faithless daughter with a sore. The prayer was also accepted, and the king noticing the sore upon his fair lady's neck, became disgusted with her and cast her off on the way.

At last the boy went within the place appointed and prayed thus: "O Merciful One, grant me two things. I wish to be a king, and I wish to be wealthy."

This prayer, however, being contrary to the directions of the faqir, was refused.

Then the wretched beggar with his recreant daughter and foolish son went on their way in the same state as they came, hungry and *pansa*less.

Sodaagaar (Merchant)

The merchants in the folklore of the region were roaming people who used to buy merchandise like ornaments, condiments, medicines, utensils, clothes, etc., from the town and then sold it to the rustic folk and the nomads. Called *sodagaar* in the folklore, they are depicted as fraudulent people who used different kinds of dupes to entice the women and children and thus swindle them. They accepted money as well as rice, maize, wheat in bargain. There are many folk tales of the region in which the *sodaagaar* is shown as beaus also for whom the country damsels had strong fascination because they used to wander from village to village and the girls on the contrary were confined to their homes. Since the *Sodaagaars* remained out of their homes most of the time, they were deceived by their wives during their absence. There are many tales in which the *soodaagaars* are cuckolded by their wives and they never come to know about their wives infidelity. Many of such tales about *soodaagaars* in Kashmir have come from Central Asia through education in Persian texts like Gulistan and Bostan of Shaikh Saidi and the works of Farid-ud Din Attar. One such tale is about a stupid merchant whose infidel wife uses different tricks to make her stupid husband believe that his wife is quite faithful. Here is a story that has come from the Persian sources.

The Stupid Merchant

> A merchant who suspected the fidelity of his wife kept a talking parrot to spy on her while he was on his usual errands. He taught the parent to say what the weather was like when the paramour of his wife visited her in his absence.
>
> The clever wife knew it.

While she enjoyed a night with her paramour, she produced artificial wind in the bed chamber and cast strong lights on the parrot's eyes. She also sprinkled a shower over the parrot.

When the merchant returned and asked the parrot about the weather, the parrot told him that there was a violent storm, thunder and lightning when the paramour visited his wife.

The merchant was convinced that the parrot lied and his wife was innocent.

Jodgar

An interesting character common to the Central Asian and Kashmiri folklore is the magician, called shaman or *jaadoogar*. The role of the magician is not only to create funny situations, but also to work as dues ex machine who can turn impossible and improbable into probable possible. The magician also cures the ailing by miraculous powers, change the external form of humans and animals, turn a human being into stone, or keep the soul imprisoned in a bird, a flower or animal. Numerous folktales and legends are centred on the magical powers of the *jadoogar* and are still very popular for the play of fantasy and imagination in them.

Thug

The thug is yet another interesting character common to Indian folklore. A thug is usually very intelligent, cunning and adept in masquerading. Only in the near past the thugs, in spite of their negative role, were an integral constituent of society and were admired for their tricks, knacks, pranks and jocular activities. They could easily swindle, disappear and re-emerge without any feeling of remorse. The thugs who showed a sense of justice in helping the needy and the helpless are most admired.

Khor (A Scald-head)

The scald-head is a recurring character in Kashmiri folk tales. He belongs to the category of the cunning characters that use different kinds of dupes to accomplish even the impossible, even elope with the princess of the country. The scald-head in a story befools even a Rantas (female monster).

The Khor and the Rantas

One day when the scald-head was seen by a Rantas in a mulberry tree eating juicy mulberries, she in the guise of an old woman asked him for a few mulberries. When the scald-head came down to put a handful of mulberries in the skirt of the Rantas, she caught hold of him and put him in her bag. On her way to her grotto, she asked a peasant to take care of the closed bag till she drank some water in a nearby stream. The scald-head cried from inside the bag, the peasant opened the bag and set the scald-head free and stuffed the bag with clods. The Rantas was disappointed when she found only clods in her bag at her home. The next day the same sequence of events was repeated, but a shepherd came to the rescue of the scald-head. The Rantas understood that she had committed a mistake. The third day she took the bag with the scald-head directly to her home and entrusted him to her daughter. The Rantas' daughter fell in love with him and hid him in a cave so that her mother did not devour him. One day while the Khor and the Rantas-girl were mincing a prey bird in a mortar, the scald-head killed her with the pestle, went inside the house, and took away all the jewels stored there by the Rantas. There are many similar tales full of the adventures of the scald-head.

Peasant

The peasants are shown as witty and sometimes inscrutable people. They have the intelligence to cheat Satan, various monsters, and even the tyrants. In Kashmiri folk tales there are hundreds to pithy sayings, called *gryiesy-ganD* (peasants' riddles) that are actual problems of measurement, guess work and wisdom. One such enigmatic *griesy-gand* is *shaal, geb ti haaki tsar* (a jackal, a sheep, and a bundle of vegetables); the question is how to carry them across a river in a boat without getting any of the three harmed. These questions are asked in childhood so that children's wit is sharpened.

Shepherd

The shepherds too belong to the wise category of characters in folktales. They too know all the tricks of duping supernatural beings and the beasts of the jungle. The shepherds are more common in the Central Asian tales and parables than those of Kashmir because they are a nomadic tribe.

Fool

The fool in folktales is not only a source of delight, but also a vehicle to carry a message against stupidity and ignorance. The fools in various styles, situations, costumes, and occupations perform the function of comic catharsis that purifies the soul from unreason, depravity, wantonness, and corruption. Other characters in the folktales may also act or behave foolishly, but the type character fool has his distinct role.

Here is a Persian fable narrated by Saidi Shirazi in his Gulstan that was taught as a text in all maktabas before the advent of modern schooling, and as such, has left an indelible effect on the folklore of Kashmir. Almost all Saidi's hikaayaats have been assimilated into Kashmiri folk literature, however with certain local nuances.

The Fool and the Donkey

A foolish man was raving at a donkey. It took no notice. A wiser man who was watching said:

> "Idiot! The donkey will never learn your language___ you should observe silence and instead master the tongue of the donkey."

Fathers and Sons

There are numerous tales in Central Asia in which the sons are shown ignoring the advice of their fathers and repenting at the end. The folklore has thus worked as an effective medium of continuation of the value of the respect for parents. Here is a tale from Uzbekistan.

Three Brothers

According to the legend, there lived one person. He had three sons. Before his death he bequeathed to his sons:

"As I shall die, let each of you three nights guards my tomb on end."

"Well", – sons had answered. A few times had passed after that, and the father had died. The senior son had gone the first night to the tomb. He had stayed at the tomb for some time as suddenly in the sky the flame had flashed. The man was frightened, had escaped to the steppe and had stayed there for three days. The turn of the second brother had come. He was frightened too and had gone somewhere for three days, and then came back home. The younger brother at last had gone to the tomb.

He saw, that in the sky the flame had lighted up and began to go down. He was frightened, but had not escaped. And the flame had suddenly started talking: "Do not be afraid. Your father had borrowed three horses from me. Now I shall return them to you. You will receive a hair from everyone and as soon as to be necessary for you a horse, burn one of them, and a horse will present before you".

The younger son took the hair and thanked him. When he had come back home, seniors said:

"We shall go on a feast to the king, and you sit at home."

"All right", answered the younger brother but as soon as the brothers went away he came to the tomb of the father and had burnt the hair of a black horse. At the very same time before him there was a black horse with black clothes for him.

The man was dressed in black clothes, sat on a horse and had gone on a feast to the *padishah* (the king).

When he arrived he saw, that the daughter of the padishah was sitting on a wall of the lock, and grooms on horses were trying to jump through a wall. He had tried, but it was not possible for him. Then he returned to a tomb of the father and burnt the hair of the black horse. He again went on a feast and once again tried to jump through a wall, and again it was not possible. Then he again returned to a tomb of the father and burnt the hair of a dun horse. The man gave a bay horse to a flame, and himself in yellow clothes on a dun horse went on a feast. That time his horse had jumped through a wall. After that he came home, he gave a horse and clothes a flame and began to wait for brothers. When they had returned, the younger brother asked them:

"What was on a feast?"

"Three times there came the unfamiliar horseman and at the third time he was successively and his horse jumped through a wall", brothers have answered.

For other day the younger brother went to gather brushwood. He collected brushwood and burnt a hair of a black horse. He sat down on it and went to a feast. He was led with all honours to a palace, different viands were brought before him. The young man looked around and saw, that his brothers stood far from a table. He sent them meat and fish. They ate and had hidden a little for the younger brother who stayed at home. Then the younger brother had imperceptibly left the feast, changed clothes and mixed with those who competed in a goat competition. He seized a goat and had thrown on a wall of the padishah's lock. The goat had fallen directly to a wall of the padishah's lock.

Then the daughter of the padishah took the younger brother for a hand and sat on a throne:

"From this time you're my husband", declared she.

And the padishah ordered to arrange a magnificent wedding. So the younger brother married the daughter of the padishah. And the padishah had soon conceded to the son-in-law a throne. He became very fair padishah. And the senior brothers returned from a feast and didn't find the younger brother at home. Then brothers begun to cry and recovered to search for him. They had heard about validity of the padishah and decided to ask him, whether he knew something about their brother.

They came to him and said:

"We had a younger brother, but we had lost him. We come to ask to help us to find him."

"If you see him, will you recognize him?" he asked them.

"Certainly."

"How did he look?"

"Your majesty, our brother was similar to you, but he had been dressed in a tatter. "

"Then know, that I am your brother. "

"How have you reached such power and happiness?"

"I had executed the will of the father and three nights slept at its tomb."

And the younger brother told to them about everything, that had happened with him. It gave brothers a horse, the senior had named the minister of the right hand, and an average – the minister of the left hand.

Thus we see there are many recurring characters in all forms of the tales and daastans in Kashmiri, each character has to play his or her dramatic role. A Dastan is a dramatic representation of collective life of a society. None of these characters evolves with time, as we see in authentic literature that emerges after the emergence of individualism in society; all these characters are names of various values and are determined by the overall value system in oral culture of a community. They are not determined by their individual actions in various conflicts, but determined and given shape by the tradition.

Stylistic Features in Folk Literature

Like the stereotyped characters in the *Dastan* we find various stylistic or technical features that are universal in folk literature. Here are some of these formal features.

a) De-Rationalisation

In the first place, every Dastan is a series of happenings in a de-rationalised setting. The narrators use many stratagems for achieving maximum de-rationalisation. The audiences are to be shifted from their mundane world of cause and effect to a distant place and remote age when all actions, highly exaggerated and impossible would sound probable. It is not without purpose that a Dastan invariably begins with words like "long long ago…", "in a city of the far East or China… there lived a king…" Thus all such tales tell us of remote places and remote times. The scene may be an island, a desert, a jungle, a hinterland, a graveyard, so on and so forth. The narrator tries his best to gain complete credibility from his audience and stimulate his fantasy and Imagination.

b) Fancy and Imagination

In order to enjoy a tale of fantasy, the listener or reader needs suspension of disbelief and has to surrender his reason to feel the significance of the myth. Though myths can evolve in our age of reason too, but most of the existing myths have evolved in primitive ages when man did not think in terms of reason, but "think" through feeling. The primitive ages can be regarded as the infancy of mankind, and infants do not know the surrounding world through cause and effect, but through forms, magnitude and physical nature. Like an infant with a pre-linguistic cognition, the primitives knew the things of the world through the significances that he/she attached to them. To the primitives every object of the physical world – flowers, stones, mountains, birds, animals, sky, stars, the sun and the moon – carried a spirit that had its own intelligence and could have human feelings. Words were not medium of communication or barriers between the thing and the human brain; and very few words were needed by the primitives. Coleridge the great English romantic poet of the nineteenth century aptly expresses human associations with the phenomenal world that exists outside the human soul.

> The intelligible forms of ancient poets,
> The fair humanities of old religion,
> The Power, the Beauty, and the Majesty
> Or forest, by slow stream, or pebbly spring.

> Or chasms and the watery depths;
> all these have vanished;
> They live no longer in the faith or reason;
> But still the hearts doth need a language; Still
> Doth the old instinct bring back the old names;
> Spirits or gods that used to share this earth
> With man as with their friend; and at this day
> 'Tis Jupitor who brings whate'er is great,
> and Venus who brings everything that's fare." [1]

It was Coleridge who gave the concepts of the "Primary and Secondary Imagination". Coleridge wrote:

> The IMAGINATION then, I consider either as primary, or secondary. The primary IMAGINATION I hold to be the living power and prime Agent of all human Perception, and as a repetition in the finite mind of the eternal act of creation in the infinite I AM. The secondary IMAGINATION I consider as an echo of the former, co-existing with the conscious will, yet still as identical with the primary in the kind of its agency, and differing only in degree, and in the mode of its operation. It dissolves, diffuses, dissipates, in order to recreate; or where this process is rendered impossible, yet still at all events it struggles to idealize and to unify. It is essentially vital, even as all objects (as objects) are essentially fixed and dead.
>
> FANCY, on the contrary, has no other counters to play with, but fixities and definites. The Fancy is indeed no other than a mode of Memory emancipated from the order of time and space; while it is blended with, and modified by the empirical phenomenon of the will, which we express by the word CHOICE. But equally with the ordinary memory of the Fancy must receive all its materials ready made from the law of association. (1907:62)

Fancy and Imagination coexist and are always at work in a living human being with a linguistic competence. Imagination, primary as well as secondary make mankind dream, plan, design and create. It gives meaning to things as associates semantic dimensions with things around. Fancy on the other hand is collective and aggregative rather than individual. It is accumulated in a community living for generations in a geographical situation. The supernatural and preternatural powers associated with visible and invisible "things" attribute human faculties to animate and inanimate things and as such have their respective souls. The primitive mind, according to Kant's philosophy, is not a passive mirror to reflect what is perceived, but an active force that influences the very shape of the perceived reality in order to arrive at truth. According to Vico, language began with gesture which in its development entered the stage of myth and figurative language. Ernest Cassirer(1923) believed that ' language and myth are "two diverse shoots from the same parent stem" that springs from the same impulse of symbolic formulation.

Man is a symbol making animal, and as such has an impulse of concentrating and heightening simple sensory experience as a result of which the primordial language originated. This primordial language was fundamentally mythic in nature. According to Susanne Langer, it was this primordial language that gave rise to all myths. In her books *Philosophy in a New Key* (1941) and *Feeling and Form* (1953) Mrs. Langer applies her theory of symbolic transformation to all forms of creative art, especially music. In her opinion music is "our myth of the inner life— a young, vital, and meaningful myth of recent inspiration and still in its 'vegetative' growth.

In Freudian psychology, myth, like poetry originates from man's faculty of dream-work. According to him, in both myth and poetry there is condensation,(accumulation of several images in one image), displacement (emergence of an unimportant element as the significant element to represent the whole and over-determination (several different significances getting coalesced to become plurisignificant). Carl Jung and other cultural anthropologists find the same kind of phenomenon happening not in one individual mind but in the collective psyche of a community and call it Collective Unconscious. The Collective Unconscious is a repository of beliefs and myths of a race that have developed through time as a result of civilisation. He termed the symbols of the Collective Unconscious as archetypes. By an archetype Jung means a primordial image which is a psychic residue of countless experiences of the same kind, and thus a part of the inherited response-pattern of the race. He made a comparative study of myths, beliefs, and rituals and thus paved a way for the analytic study of the material of the Collective unconscious in an objective way. The sum total of his study was the universals in apparently diverse myths and archetypes.

CHAPTER 2

Origin and Development of *Dastangoi* in Kashmir

For its unique geographical position Kashmir has been a meeting place and watershed of many cultures, languages, folklore, and religions. No date can be fixed for the emergence of the first habitation in Kashmir, but, on the bases of the archaeological remains and the nature of the land with fertile land and plenty of all the requirements of human life, mankind must have existed from the Palaeolithic times. The earliest human dwellings must have existed on various table lands, around the primeval lake called Sati Sar in Hindu lore. The remains at Burzahama, Gophakral, Ahrabal, Hirapore, Mattan, Zainapora, Damoodar, Lar, Pattan, Kreri, Bandipore, Pampore, Divsar, Bonyaar, Tangamarg and other plateaus suggest that human habitation must have existed on the upper reaches of the valley before the water of the legendary lake, later called Sati Sar in Hindu lore, found a vent through the gorge at Kahadanyaar in the north-west mountains. The story element in the folklore of Kashmir, therefore starts with the very coming into existence of the valley. The story is as old as mankind in the valley, but was later rendered into a long poem called the *Neelamatapurana*, written in the ninth or tenth century.

The Neelamatapurana

The story of the *Neelamatapurana*, that suggests the lake origin of the valley, was a prehistoric story and has much in common with other stories of lake origin of different countries. The legend says that Kashmir was a huge mountainous lake for six Manvantras or Mnuvantaras (= Manu + antara; =306,720,000 x 6 human years). The legend says that after the end of six *manuantaras*, in the *pera* of the seventh Manu, a demon called *Jal-ud-bhava* (born in water) appeared in the lake from the semen of a *rakhshasa* (demon) named *Sangrah* who lived on the tops of the Himalayas. One day when he could not overpower Parvati in molesting her, his semen dropped into the lake which bred the ferocious Jal-adbhava which was by birth immortal until he remained peaceful and pious. But the demon forgot his promise and started devouring the Nagas, the humans living in the nearby mountains. The king of the Nagas supplicated to a pious rishi, namely Kashyapa Rishi who was endowed with miraculous powers. He, with the help of Vishnu and his brother Bakabhadra, caused a rent in the enclosing mountains of the lake at Khadanyaar, the water of the lake receded making the gigantic Jaladbhawa visible; Vishnu eventually killed the demon. In the text of the *Neelamatapurana* the following lines sum up the whole sequence of events:

Navdehan sati devi bhumibharvati parthiv
Tasyan tu bhumav bhavti sarstu vimlodkam;
Shadyojannayatam ramyam taddhern cha visttrtam
Satideshshmiti khyatam devakridam manoharam. (45-46)

Tr. The goddess Sati, with the body in the form of the boat, became the earth and on that earth comes into being a lake of clear water, known as Satidesha, six yojanas long and half of that in breadth, enjoyable, heart enrapturing, and the sporting place. (Kumari, Dr. Ved. Tr. *Neelamatapurana,* Vol. ii, Srinagar: The Jammu and Kashmir Academy of Art, Culture and Languages. 1973, p. 12

The land in the form of a valley was then settled by human population with the help of Kashyapa. In view of the animosity between the two hostile clans, that is the aborigines Nagas and the Dards coming from the north-west, Kashyapa acted as a mediator and made them reach an agreement that the during the six months of spring the valley would be inhabited by the Nagas and for the six months of summer the Dards, also known as the Pashachas in Sanskrit lore.

Hieymaal – Naagraay

The tale of *Hieymaal–Naagraay,* another indigenous folk-tale of Kashmir has been rendered into many versions of *Dastans* and is still one of the most popular *Dastan.* The story is certainly an allegorical version of the historical event of synthesis between the Nagas and the Pashachas or later Sarasvatis. The story revolves around the tragic story of the two central characters, Hieymaal and Naaagraay. The former is the daughter of a Dard, named Baavir, living in the village of Balapore located on the tableland near Shopian and Naagraay, the prince of the Nagas or serpents of the underworld. One day Balavir, being tired of walking, and also fed up of his nagging wife, had a sweet nap near a spring of the bank of the river Rimbara. Meanwhile a serpent sneaked into Balavir's luggage. When he woke up he saw the snake in his luggage, he closed its mouth with a rope and thought of taking it home so that it bit his wicked wife and get freedom from her. He took the luggage and walked towards his home. He placed the bag in his shanty and closed the outer door and walked away to while away for some time. After some time he returned, opened the door, and calmly walked in. To his amazement, he finds a handsome prince in front of his wicked wife who was laughing boisterously. The prince tells him that his name is Naegraay and being fed up with his wives he came out from his abysmal land to see the charms and freedom of the world on the surface of the earth. He further tells them that he wants to live with them; he is allowed to stay in their shanty.

One day the prince Naagraay, in the disguise of a common man accompanies Balavir to his spring where he happens to see his daughter. The two fall in love with each other. The wedding is performed with full celebrations.

Many days after their marriage, a girl-friend of Naagraay's earlier wives, comes to the village in search of Naagraay. She is disguised as a woman pot-vendor. She visits their house. On her very first glance at Naagraay, she recognises him and tells Hiemal that she knows his earlier wives. However, he tells her that he is a poor scavenger of their village. Hearing this, Hiemaal is deeply shocked and when Naagraay returns in the evening, Hiemaal asks him to confirm what his actual caste is. Naagraay tries his best to console Hiemaal that he is faithful to her and has forgotten his earlier wives, Hiemall persists to urge him to reveal to her his actual caste. In order to test his nature and caste, she arranges for a big bowl of milk and asks him to dive into that jar of milk. Naagraay prevaricates, but the stubborn Hiemaal makes him undergo the test. The wicked woman who visited their house in the guise of a woman pot-vendor, grabs the chance and drags Naagraay down to his house in the underworld. Hiemaal is left in utter grief and wailing. She seeks the help of the spiritual powers of a Faqir and succeeds in making way to reach the underworld of Paataal and meet her estranged love. Nagraay takes pity on her distressed soul and gives her shelter in his house as a maid.

She lives as a maid servant in the house and works day and night to keep the kindred of Naagraay happy. But one day per chance the young ones of Naagraay receive burns when the pot full of simmering rice water tumbles. They bite Hiemal and she falls unconscious because of the venom. Naagraay sends her for treatment. After thorough treatment at Yariwan (Forest of Pines), she recovers and regains her former beauty. In the meantime a rich merchant sees her and falls in love with her. He abducts her to some unknown hiding place. The aggrieved Naagraay makes a thorough search to find her and after many travails finally manages to reach that hiding place. He assumes his original shape of a serpent and sits curled around her. When the merchant returns to his house and finds a huge serpent sitting curled around his love, he draws his sword and cuts the body of the snake into pieces. When Hiemaal wakes up and finds Naagraay in a pool of blood, she wails a lot. The dismembered body of Naagraay is taken to Hiemaal's native village Balapore where the body is placed on a pyre of wood for cremation. Hiemaal too plunges into the flames and is consumed in the fire. The two lovers get reincarnated as two springs: the spring of Hiemaal and the Spring of Naagraay; the waters of the two springs flow into the river of Rimbara.

Thus we see how the folk memory of Kashmir has preserved the memory of the Naagas and the Dards in the form of a sweet but sad tale of the supernatural. There is no history in the tale, but it certainly intimates the synthesis of two different races, nevertheless in the form of the supernatural events.

The early folk beliefs were grounded in the concept of the evanescent nature of the soul and the transience of material forms. They believed that the soul can easily have free will to take any material form, but never perishes itself. The notion of this change, called metempsychosis in folk lore studies, appears in many *Dastan*s of perennial fascination. Here is the tale of a parrot narrated by Wahab Khar, a famous Sufi poet of the nineteenth century. The tale by its very essence is as old as the folklore of Kashmir. Wahab Khar has given it a literary form. Here is the Dastan in translation.

Tale of a Parrot

This is what my Master told me:

> There was a certain country, the land of Persia, and it was ruled by a king named Bahadur Khan. He had many gardens for his womenfolk, into

which no stranger was allowed to enter; but once there came into it a Faqir. The discerners then discerned him, and the newsmen gave the news to the King. They said, "A Faqir has come into the garden. The King heard, and took with him his Vizir. To the garden they went, and there he saw the Faqir.

"O Faqir, how didst thou enter? Where dost thou belong?

Whence art thou come?"

The Faqir said,

I came only for a stroll. What of yours have I eaten?

Hark ye, loyalty is monstrous rare.

It chanced that before the king there was a flowering plant, and at its foot a dead nightingale. As soon as they spoke angrily to the Faqir, he fell flat, lifeless to the ground, and as he did so the nightingale arose alive. Such magic power did he show the king. The nightingale flew out of the garden, and returned. Then it fell dead and the Faqir again became alive. He began to depart, but they entreated him saying:-

O Faqir, let me be thy servant!

Cups of the cream of mlk will I fill for thee.

Special pulaos and delicacies wilt thou not eat?

Hark ye, loyalty is monstrous rare.

So the Faqir confided the secret of his magic power to the King, and the King confided it to his Vizir.

The King gave instructions to the Vizir, and he thus became proficient in the secret.

They went out hunting together.

Hark ye, loyalty is monstrous rare.

In the forest they saw a parrot dead,

"O vizir, how beautiful this must have been.

Put thou, I beseech thee, thy life into it but for a moment."

Hark ye, loyalty is monstrous rare.

Said the Vizir:

"My King, for long hath it been dead.

A stink cometh from it; who knoweth when it died?

Hark ye, loyalty is monstrous rare.

For this did the King make urgent entreaty to the Vizir. "Fain would I see how beautiful the parrot was," but the Vizir refused to listen to him.

And, further, my master told me:

In his heart their was treachery. At length the King himself abandoned his own body and entered into the parrot. Up rose the parrot, and flew about. Then the Vizir did a deed: he himself entered into the King's body. What was what had all along been in his heart.

The burden which had been the King's to bear,

That became laid upon the foolish Vizir.

Treachery was watching in him like a petitioner.

Hark ye, loyalty is monstrous rare.

The parrot is flying in the air, and the Vizr is in the body of the King. He stood up.

He mounted the King's horse and went into the army. He sad to them:-

"The Vizir fell from his horse and is dead.

That was the news that the newsman brought.

Hark ye, loyalty is monstrous rare.

When this Vizir had done the deed, and when he had entered the King's body, in his hand had he raised his sword, and into small pieces did he cut his own dead body. Then said he to his army. "Go forth, ye archers, and ye gunmen. Whoever of you killeth a parrot, to him will be given a reward. "When the parrot heard this order, he fled afar, and went to the Faqir, who on that day had been in his garden.

He gave the order to the archers.

"Pay ye heed, I pray, to my coaxing."

He gave an order that the parrot should be killed.

Hark ye, loyalty is monstrous rare.

Now, as for the real king, he was in the parrot, and had taken refuge with the Fair; so that the parrot was not killed by anyone. One day the Vir-King sallied forth to hunt.; and when he had reached a certain place he decried a hind. After it they made pursuit. They brought it into the army, and he said to them. "I will cut off the head of him who letteth her escape.

And, further, my Master told me:

But the hind gave a sudden spring and leaped over the head of the Vizir-king himself. They pursued her Now the parrot King was with the Faqir, and that Faqir was a magician clairvoyant. Quoth he to the Parrot-King. "Go forth, your Majesty, today wilt thou regain thine own body." Meanwhile the hind had far outdistanced her pursuers.

Furthermore, my Master told me:

> There there lay a dead bear. The Vizir –King entered into the bear and pursued the hind., leaving the real King's body lying on the ground.
>
> The news of the Vizir-King's coming was heard by the parrot. Thither did he run.
>
> He waited, watching from a tree-hole.
>
> He again entered into his own body;
>
> wish ye him all good luck!
>
> Hark ye, loyalty is monstrous rare.
>
> Down fell the parrot dead, and the King entered his own body, but he who had been the Vizir was now in the bear. The real King mounted his horse, and said to his men. "Shoot ye that bear." They fired with their guns at him, and broke his leg. They seized him and brought him before the King. Said the King, "Treachery was done by thee to me. What can I do but kill thee? Otherwise people will say of me, ' He hath a bear for a Vizir.' Thou hast destroyed thine own body. Now no longer can I keep a bear like thee as a Vizir. Sir, I am about to kill thee."

And my Master further said:

> They brought firewood, and they burnt the Vizir to ashes.
>
> A hundred years passed, less or more.
>
> And then came the messenger of death to Bahadur Khan.
>
> O Wahab*, the blacksmith, cried "Allah, Allah"
>
> Hark ye, loyalty is monstrous rare.

The belief in the possibility of the external soul in animals is a recurring theme in all the folklore of Central Asia. The Shmans of Central Asia are believed to make use of this magical prowess in keeping their soul, or one of their souls, safe in the body of some animal. Frazer wrote about the notion of the external soul prevalent in Central Asia:

> 'Nobody can find my external soul,' said one famous wizard, 'it lies hidden far away in the stony mountains of the Edzhigansk.' Only once a year, when the last snow melts and the earth turns black, do these external souls of wizards appear in the shape of animals among their dwellings. They wander everywhere, yet none but wizards can see them. The strong ones weep roaring and noisily, the weak steal about quietly and furtively. Often they fight, and then the wizard whose external soul is beaten falls ill or dies. The weakest and the most cowardly wizards are they whose souls are incarnate in the shape of dogs, for the dog gives his human double no peace, but gnaws his heart and tears his body. The most powerful wizards are they whose external souls have the shape of stallions, elks, black bears,

> eagles, or boars. Again, the Samoyeds of the Turukhinsk region hold that every shaman has a familiar spirit in the shape of a boar, which he leads about by a magic belt. On the death of the boar the shaman himself dies. (4-12.)

In Kashmir, too, it is widely believed that an adept magician can transfix any human being or an animal in a pebble, a rock, a tree and the like. There are numerous tales in which the *jaadoogars* are shown with the power of petrifying a human being. Some stories even say that some of the big boulders are petrified people of the past and can come into life when the period of the punishment expires.

Human sacrifice is perhaps the most awful of all the totems. Though there is no evidence of human sacrifice in Kashmir and Central Asia, but there are certain folktales in which killing one's own dearest son for the joy of a Yogi or Pir is a recurring universal theme. In Kashmir the Story of *Akanandun* is one such story that has remained one of the most popular stories ever heard. Though it will be a travesty of the story to give it in summary as it is its structure of the narrative that is the secret of the charm of the story, yet it is worthwhile here.

There lived an old Brahman couple in a remote village of Kashmir. They had everything but lived a miserable life as they did not have a son. They performed all rituals to please their God to get a male issue, but all proved futile.

One day a Yogi with queer brightness in his eyes and in a negligee entered their house and asked for alms. The husband and wife gave the Yogi alms to his complete satisfaction. The Yogi was happy with them and asked them why they looked so sad. They revealed the cause of their suffering to the Yogi.

The Yogi closed his eyes for a while and then opened them. He laughed boisterously. "Why do you laugh? Tell us the secret O pitiless Yogi." The old Brahmin asked the Yogi.

"You are destined to have a son, but there is one condition," the Yogi told them.

"Yes, we are ready to fulfil all conditions however difficult and painful it might be."

"You shall have a son as pretty as the sun. Your life shall be filled with joy. He shall bloom into his teens, but then…" The Yogi stopped and began to pant.

"Then what ?" asked the old men with pallor on their wrinkled faces. "Tell us what is going to happen next?"

"You shall have to kill your own son and offer his flesh to me. Now tell me are you ready?"

The old couple shed tears and could not utter a word in reply.

"Tell me shall you still yearn for the son?"

"Yes, yes O heartless Yogi, we are ready. Let us have the bliss of a son of our own."

"You shall have a son pretty as the sun," saying this the Yogi vanished into thin air.

After nine months the wife of the Brahmin gave birth to a son as pretty as the sun. The child was named Akanandun. The house of the old couple was filled with joy. The father, the mother and their daughters nursed the child with all possible care. So absorbed they were in their glee that they did not even remember the Yogi's condition. Year after year passed till the boy was twelve.

One sunny afternoon when Akanandun was in his school, the Yogi with the same awesome brightness in his eyes and ruffled hair and in a negligee appeared in their house. The old couple shivered with fear. They sent one of their daughters to the school to keep Akanandun engaged in play so that the Yogi did not see him.

"Where is Akanandun, my child? I am feeling hungry."

This made the old couple cry loudly as if they wailed. But the Yogi was not moved, he guffawed in his usual way.

"O heartless Yogi, have pity on us. Do not snatch away our life from us. We shall offer you all dainties to quell your hunger, but spare the life of our son."

All screaming and wailing had no effect on the laughing Yogi.

Then with heavy hearts, Akanandun was brought home. The Yogi's face brightened to see the child. He caressed the child and then asked his parents to get him a knife. The agonised parents got him the knife. The Yogi killed the boy, dismembered his body and cut all parts into smaller pieces. He put all the flesh into a pot and began to cook it.

When the flesh of the child was toughly cooked, the Yogi put it in plates, one for each inmate of the house. The father and mother watched him doing all this eyes aghast with horror. On the goading of the Yogi, they took their plates in their hands. There was still a plate full of the cooked flesh and there was no other person to have it. "Who is the other person to have that extra plate ?

"Akanandun, who else?" The Yogi said.

The bereaved couple wailed loudly to hear the Yogi's reply.

"Yes, it is for Akanandun, my dearest child. Call him in." The Yogi did not show any compassion.

"I say call Akanandun. He shall partake of this delicious food," the Yogi said sternly.

"Akanandun, my soul, where are you? Come on in. The yogi wants you." The mother called her son loudly but in a mournful voice.

Akanandun anon romped in, as bright as usual. They bereaved couple knew no bounds with joy to see their son unharmed. All were taken aback to see him there. They hugged him one by one and then looked towards the Yogi. He had disappeared again in thin air.

The boy Akanandun grew into a handsome young man and made his parents and other kindred happy.

This story descended down to us from the remote past is reminiscent of the Aryans among whom human sacrifice prevailed. It has many parallels in Central Asian folklore and in Islamic history. The sacrifice stands for man's complete surrender before God's will and vanquishing desire and greed.

Besides numerous tales and long narratives that emerged in the local population, there are numerous tales that the people borrowed from other nations and amalgamated them into their folk memory. The folk literature of Central Asia has greatly influenced the literature. The influence of Central Asian folklore and folk literature on that of Kashmir through creative literature started in the fourteenth century, but it was in the early eighteenth century that the influence was more profound and deep-rooted. It was Mir Abdullah Baihaqi (Srinagar: d. 1807) who initiated translation or adaptation of Persian classics into Kashmiri verse.[10]

His ancestors had migrated to Kashmir in the fourteenth century from Baihaq in the time of Sultan Sikander. G.M.D.Sufi writes:

Soon after the accession, Ali Shah put an end to all feuds among his nobles. He appointed Sayyid Muhammad Mubarak Baihaqi, who was a Sunni, as his prime minister. Sayyid Muhammad Mubarak Baihaqi was the grandson of Sayyid Muhammad Baihaqi whom we knew in the course of the struggle between Muhammad Shah and Fateh Shah. Sayyid Muhammad Mubarak was the son of Sayyid Ibrahim Baihaqi, the father-in-law of Bad Shah and had migrated to Kashmir during the time of Sultan Sikandar from Baihaq, a district to the North West of Nishapur in Iran. They took a very prominent part in the politics of Kashmir during the days of the later Shah-Mirs. (225)

Baihaqi's translation of *Sheikh San'an, Qisa-I Musa,* and *Sangtaraash* had a deep impact on the collective consciousness of the Kashmiri people as the translations were immediately popular. There are numerous folk songs in which the characters and episodes of these legends occur.

In the legend of Sangtaraash a god-fearing sculptor of Kohi-Tuur makes a stony icon of God and keeps the icon on a citadel in a temple.

He worships the icon all the time and observes all rules of abstinence. One day while the devotee was away on some chore, Prophet Moses passed by the temple. He demolished the temple and broke the icon. On this act of anger on the devotee's naivety, God sent him His word of disapproval through Gabriel.

Mir Abdullah Baihaqi sermonises thus:

Haay luukoo saaryi khwati chhuv lool jaan
Looli siityiy zuv chhu laban musta'aan
Mir Abdullah chhu mangaan dwah ti raath
Lool eshqun tyiy dyitas ay paak zaat[12]

(Tr. O people love is more precious than anything else
It is love that God gets His existence;
Mir Abdullah prays day and night,
"O God bestow true love on him!")

The transfer of Central Asian legends into Kashmiri continued in the nineteenth and the twentieth century and thus Kashmiri folk literature got enriched. Here is a mention of some more popular legends of Central Asia in Kashmiri folk literature.

Zain al-Arab is the daughter of K'ab, the king of Qasdar, a city in ancient Afghanistan. She is exceptionally beautiful and a poet. K'ab receives several proposals for his daughter who is exceptionally beautiful. But her father wants o get her married to an equally good and heroic husband and thus rejects all proposals. Meanwhile K'ab dies, but before his death he advises his only son Harith to fulfil his wish.

On the occasion of his coronation, Harith receives guests from all the friendly countries. Harith has a servant, named Baktash, who is a beautiful and proficient musician. Baktash is ordered to sing for the delight of the guests. Hearing his song, Zain al-Arab falls in love with Baktash.

Zain al-Arab does not reveal her love for Baktash and pines inwardly. Harith seeks help from all the physicians, but nothing cures Zain al-Arab. Ultimately she divulges her secret to her most intimate maid. The maid takes her message to Baktash and he too begins to burn in the passion for her. Zain al-Arab composes beautiful love songs and sends them to Baktash who sings them.

One night Baktash somehow manages to enter the bed chamber of Zain al-Arab and implores for a night's pleasue. But Zain al-Arab tells her that her love is chaste and free from carnal desires. On Baktashes persistent effort, Zain al-Arab flees. The two lovers thus bear the pangs of separation, the essence of true love. Meanwhile the king of Qandhaar attacks Balakh. King Harith applies all his power to defend his country from the invader. Baktash who like other countrymen fights the invading army, is seriously wounded. Zain al-Arab, disguised as a male soldier comes to the rescue of Baktash and saves him, without letting him know her identity. Amir-I Nasr, the king of Bukhara joins Harith against the invaders. Rudki, the great poet of Central Asia, was the poet laurete of the King of Bukhara. The invaders are defeated and the there is great festivity in the country.

During the victory celebrations, Rudki meets Zain al-Arab. The two poets compete in versification and Rudki memorises some of her verses. The guests depart.

Many days after this, Amir Nasr invites Harith Shah. Rudki, on the insistence of his master, sings some of the songs of Zain al-Arab. Amir Nasr is much delighted to hear some new songs. Rudki tells his master that the songs are not his composition but that of Zain al-Arab. Amir Nasr gets impatient to see Zain al-Arab, but Rudki tells him that she is an immoral woman who loves a serf called Baktash. Harith Sha is infuriated to hear this, and in order to set things right, returns to his country. Baktash is arrested, and put into a dark abyss. Zain al-Arab is also imprisoned in a hot Hamam (a chamber kept by steam). She suffers all the pain of simmering heat and confinement and writes her pathetic songs of separation on the walls of the Hamaam. She eventually dies. After her burial, Baktash is released from the dark hole. When the news of Zain al-Arab's death is broken to him, he in fit of wrath stabs Harith Shah to death. He sings mournful songs at the grave of his beloved and slays himself at the spot.

The tragic legend of Zain al-Arab, a part of Kashmiri folklore was been rendered into the form of a *mathnavi* by Abdul Ahad Nazim (Bijbihara, Kashmir: 1816-1851).[13]

In the famous city of Nakhshab of Persia, there lived a prince, called Maasum Shah, who was the only son of the king, named Faghfuur. One day while taking delight of a musical concert, Maasuum Shah descried a strange bird in the tree near his window. The bird was so attractive that the prince longed to catch it and put it in a golden cage. His courtiers tried to dissuade him, but he was so furious that he stood up and began shaking his body. As a result of this a few pearls got detached from his crown and fell on the carpet. The queer bird in the tree anon came down to peck at the pearls. The courtiers thus knew what the bird ate. They set a snare and spread pearls over it. The bird was caught in the snare. The prince was so engrossed in the strange habits of the bird that he continued gazing at it.

After a few days the bird in the cage stopped taking any food and looked morose. Seeing this, the prince grew anxious and wanted to know the reason. When the bird saw the prince in distress, it started narrating its tale of woe. The bird told the prince that it could make him happy had it been in its original form. But also it had undergone metempsychosis under a curse.

The bird tells the prince that she is essentially a princess, called Noshlab and belonged to a country called Baitul Aman. Her father's name is Mashhoor Shah and her mother's name is Gulbadan. The bird further tells the prince that a prince of Turkistan, named Ajab Malik was in love with her as he had heard the praises of her beauty through a traveller. Ajab Malik had abdicated the palace and set out on a sea journey in search of her. He was accompanied by many friends of his, but his ship was wrecked in the ocean. Everyone perished in the sea, except Ajab Malik who sailed on a piece of the broken ship and reached an island where he discovered a Pari imprisoned in a grotto. He had set her free by killing the monster who had eloped with her. The name of the Pari was Nazmast, who was none other than a close friend of Noshlab.

Thus Noshlab, in the shape of the encaged bird, continues to narrate that her friend Nazmast came to know the identity of Ajab Malik and his problem. She managed to arrange for a meeting between Noshlab and Ajab Malik in a garden. The lover and beloved, thus united consummated their desire and promised to live a married life. Noshlab further tells the prince that while she was busy making love with her lover in the garden and quenching her carnal desire, her mother descried her in that awkward condition. While the lover and the beloved were in deep slumber, her mother in rage got Ajab Malik, the love-lorn prince, arrested and exiled him to Turkistan while he was asleep. Noshlab too in her slumber was taken away and kept confined in her bed chamber in the palace. Noslab, when awake, yelled and wept, but her mother did not take pity on her. She on the contrary cast a spell on her and changed her into a bird to wander about. She had been in the form of a bird for twenty long years and flew from country to country in search of her love, Ajab Malik.

Maasuum Shah thus knew the secret of the queer bird and took the encaged bird to Baitul Aman. He persuaded the parents of Ajab Mailk to arrange the marriage of Ajab Malik and Noshlab.

After a series of interesting episodes and twists in the story, Nosh Lab get transformed into her original human form and her marriage is finalised with Ajab Malik. Eventually Maasuum Shah, too, gets married with the bosom friend of Noshlab. Ajab Malik's friend Rasikh also finds a bride, Mastnaz, the younger sister of Nazmast. All the reunited lovers happily return to their respective countries.

The legend of Gulrez is the most popular tale in Kashmiri because of its beautiful poetic rendering by a late nineteenth century poet Maqbool Shah (Kraalawor, Kashmir: (?-d. 1877). It may be pointed out here that the original Persian tale is in prose, recorded by Zia Nakhshabi [14]

The romance concerns the love story of Bahram, the only son of the king of Baglana. His love affair starts from his school in which the daughter of the Vazir of the country; her name is Zuhra. The Vazir did not like Bahram's advances towards his daughter at that tender age and thus stopped her from attending that school. He also complained to the king that his son had seduced his innocent daughter. The king in his rage ordered the prince's exile.

Bahram used his old maid servant in sending a secret message to Zuhra. She helps Zuhra leave her father's house secretly in the morning and run off with Behram towards a desert.

The Vazir orders his men to follow the fleeing lovers and get the Prince arrested. The exhausted eloped lovers reach an oasis and they come down from the horse to rest. Zuhra eventually falls asleep and Behram remains guarding her. A lion attacks them, but the prince valiantly fights the lion, chases it and finally kills it at a distance. Zura wakes up, finding no trace of the prince there, she rides towards the desert in search of him. Meanwhile, Behram returns to the spot, and finding no trace of Zura there, is much perturbed. The two lovers thus set out in two directions in search of each other.

After several days of a solitary journey, Zuhra reaches a beautiful garden of a country and wants to have a sojourn there. The prince of that country chances to see her in the garden and falls in live with her at first sight. But Zuhra does not reciprocate and tells the prince of the country she is a wayfarer, detached from her caravan and that her name is Khirdmand. The prince invites her to his palace and arranges a feast in her honour.

At night the prince and his friends get drunk and assault Zuhra. The latter bravely defends her chastity and runs away carrying the prince's crown on her head.

Zuhra, disguised as a man, reaches another country and takes refuge in the house of a woman. She tells her host that "he" was a merchant, "his" caravan was looted by pirates and "he" managed to save "his" life. Zurha disguised as a young man stayed in the country. The fame of her beauty spread all around and the princess of the country fell in love with her, passed as a young man. Zuhra, too, continued to retain her disguise.

One day she, disguised as a young man, on the pretext of hunting, comes out of the country so that she could search for her lost lover, Behram. A king of yet another country sees her (him). He likes him / her and, having no son of his own, offers her/him to be his son. Zuhra reflects and for certain gains accepts the king's offer. The king wants to get his only daughter married to her/him. Zuhra somehow convinces the king to postpone the marriage for one year. Meanwhile the king dies and she (as the adopted son) ascends the throne.

One day, while on an errand of hunting, Zuhra (now disguised as the new king) chances to find a young man, but worn out and emaciated. She recognises him as her own lover Behram. Zuhra orders her men to carry Behram to the palace where she arranges for energising food and regal robes for him. She then reveals her true self to Behram. She gets married to her lover. The actual princess of the country goes mad to see this, but Zuhra being magnanimous, allows Behram to have her as a second wife. Behram thus becomes the prince of a new country.

The story of Zura and Behram is full of funny and dramatic twists. The whole interest lies in the mistaken identity of Zuhra, as male and as female. Mistaken identity of people is yet another recurring theme of Central Asian legends and folk tales.

The haunting story of *Shirin wa Khusrav* has been a popular legend in Kashmir since Mehmood Gami (Memoodabad: 1755-1850) adapted it from Abu'r Rahman Jami's *mathnavi* of the same title.

Khusrav Parvez is the only son of Hurmuz, the son of Navshirvan of Iran. He has been born to his parents after many religious rituals and prayers and offerings at various shrines. Khusrav Parvez grows up as a young man of unparalleled beauty. In his early teens he happens to hear about the virtues and beauty of Shireen, the daughter of a rich lady of Arman. The praises of Shireen silently move Khurav Parvez to uncontrollable love for the paragaon of beauty, Shireen. He eventually sends Shahvoor, his friend to Arman to persuade Shireen to visit his palace.

Shahvoor stealthily enters Shireen's garden and keeps a portrait of Khusrav hanging on a tree there. When Shireen sees the portrait she grows crazy seeing the bewitching beauty of Khusrav Parvez. She asks Shahvoor the address of Khusrav Parvez and Shavoor gives her a ring of Khusrav Parvez so that she could find him easily.

Riding her horse, named Shabdez, Shireen travels to Khusrav Parvez's country. Meanwhile, Khusrav Parvez's minister Behram maligns him before his father who is enraged. Khusrav Parvez runs away from his palace and takes refuge in Shiree's house in Arman. When Shireen reaches Khusrav Parvez's palace, she shows his parents the ring that was sent to her. She is well treated there. Meanwhile Khusrav Parvez's father dies and he returns to his country and ascends the throne. During this time, Shireen returns to her home, where she does not find Khusrav Parvez.

Behram, Khusrav Parvez's the minister becomes a rebel and makes Khusrav Parvez flee his country. He again takes refuge in Shireen's house at Arman. Sheerin motivates Khusrav Parvez to take revenge on Behram and recover his power. Khusrav Parvez follows her advice and attacks Behram and defeats him. He assumes the rule of his country. In the meantime, Shireen's mother also dies and Shireen assumes power. Khusrav Parvez sends his friend Shavor to get Shireen for him.

A parallel story emerges when a stone-cutter, named *Farhaad* or *Kohkan* (= stone cutter) emerges as another ardent lover of Shireen. Shireen's only diet is milk of goats, but it would take a very long time to fetch milk from the pastures that are located behind a hill, called Beestone. Khusrav Parvez, therefore, orders Farhaad the stone-cutter to dig a channel across the hill so that milk flows through it to Shireen's palace. Since Farhad the stone-cutter, though convinced of the stupendous ordeal, accepts the challenge to give expression to the ardour of his love for Shireen; he digs the channel. But he demands Shireen as a reward for the accomplishment. Khusrav Parvez in his perplexity spreads a rumour that Shireen has died suddenly. On hearing this rumour, Farhad in a fit of shock kills himself with his own hammer. Shireen is much bereaved at the sad end of her ardent lover. However, she lives with Khusrav Parvez.

Khusrav Parvez has a son by his earlier wife. He imprisons him and then kills him. Shireen in her distress commits suicide.

The tragic story of Khusrav Parvez and Shireen, also know as the story of Shiree wa Farhaad has become an integral part of Kashmiri folk literature. There are numerous songs in which the allusion of Shireen and Farhaad occur that signify the purity of passionate love.[15]

The tale has been rendered into mathnavis by Mehmood Gami. After him, the tale was also rendered into a drama by Ghulam Nabi Dilsoz in the fifth decade of the twentieth century.

The impact of all these Central Asian tales, legends and dastans on the collective life of Kashmiri people has been manifold. The fictional romantic characters of these Dastans and the phantasmagoria associated with them gradually left deep and indelible impressions on the collective psyche of the masses who heard them time and again. Kashmiri culture at all levels accepted influence from the romantic grandeur: social etiquette, modes of address, styles of dress, concepts of delicacies, methods of cooking, variety of niceties in food, entertaining the guests, household appliances _____ every aspect of Kashmiri culture now savours and reminds us of Central Asian culture. Take, for instance, this popular marriage song:

shoqi chaanyi vaayay chang wa nay saazoo
aakhoo shahryey shhyieraazoo
hoori chhay vanivaan nuuri mahaaraazo
aakhoo shahryey shhyieraazoo
maayi chaanyi gur ti gwond puuri swani saazoo
taazun chyoon layi lachh tyi zyaday
woaDyi chhuy shimli ti neely pyeshwaazoo
aakhoo shahryey shhyieraazoo
tsiy chhukh yazman chyoon mahaaraazoo
tsaakhoo leelyi hindyi darvaazoo
leel chhay peeryith swarmi ti saazoo
aakhoo shahryey shhyieraazoo
leelyi hindyi maalyinyi bah shath vaazoo
taazi taazi nyaamets raninaavaan
saaliry siity chhyiy puuryi andaazoo
aakhoo shahryey shhyieraazoo
wathirun kormay manz roobi khaanas
leel myarjaanyi ti majnuunas
majnuun chhuy gyinadaan narday baazoo
aakhoo shahryey shhyieraazoo
ath dyievaankhaanas bah darvaazoo
Shah Sultaan yetyi gah traavaan
suy gash sari kar haa ayaazoo
aakhoo shahryey shhyieraazoo

(Tr. In ecstasy, we shall sing and play the chang and flute,
you have entered the city of Sheeraaz.
The nymphs of paradise sing for you O darling bridegroom.
you have entered the city of Sheeraaz.
For our love for you we have adorned the horse with golden saddle, your turban made of golden fibre is priceless.
Your head-dress is shimla and your robe is a peshwaazah,
you have entered the city of Sheeraaz.
O bride's father the bridegroom is yours,
You have entered the gates of Laila's palace.
Laila is adorned in numerous ornaments,
you have entered the city of Sheeraaz.
Twelve hundred cooks are engaged
in preparing hundreds of dainties;
the guests, too, are adorned in royal style.
I have laid cushions in the guest-room
for you and your bride, Laila.
But Majnuun is still absorbed in childish pranks
you have entered the city of Sheeraaz.

> The guest room has as many as twelve hunded doors,
> And Shah Sultun sits there in full grandeur,
> O Ayaaz, you know the significance of that light,
> you have entered the city of Sheeraaz.)

This immortal marriage song composed by one of our lyrical Sufi poets adequately reflects various facets of Kashmir's cultural life that have undergone complete transformation in accordance with the culture of Central Asian countries.

Before the advent of modern electronic media, there was a specific vocation in Kashmir to sing these *Dastan*s and the roaming entertainers used to sing the *Dastan*s in villages and towns to earn a livelihood. They were generally called Shaairs (poets); Walter Lawrence recognises them as a special professional class. He writes:

> ...They are either minstrels who sing to the accompaniment of a guitar, or the village poets, who suddenly spring up in the midst of business and recite in a loud shrill tone the praises of the most influential person present. I knew many of these poets, and have spent many hours listening patiently to rhymes which seemed to have no end, and which jumbled up in a curious manner oriental tropes with the most commonplace and technical terms of survey and revenue work. It is good to give these poets a few rupees, for they are often miserably poor. (235)

With the advent of modern modes of entertainment, the *Dastan* singers, too, have changed their profession. They have adjusted their art in conformity with the demands of radio and television. There are many *Dastango* (professional singers of *Dastan)* who are very popular in singing the legends of Central Asia, discussed above. The Dastan singers enjoyed tremendous popularity, almost adoration, in Kashmir till recent times. They were invited to recite the tales of romance, adventure and wars and each *Dastan* was recited usually in several instalments. The singers of the past wandered from street to street and village to village and when they chose a proper spot, usually crossroads, threshing ground or an open space, played on their *saarangi* to invite crowds and then sang the tales with interludes of prose narration.

CHAPTER 3

Use of Performing Arts in Presenting a Tale

The genre of *Dastan* is a complete and composite art that includes many other forms of narration, representation, communication and entertainment. In this respect the study of the *Dastan* involves study of all these elements as integral parts of the *Dastan.* With the role of the central figure, the impresario, the performer, communicator, and interpreter, the narrator is the soul and strength of the art form. He has to be master of all those forms that go into the making of a particular *Dastan*; the ratio and interrelationship of the components, however, varies from *Dastan* to *Dastan.* It is again the narrator who is the sole judge of integrating diverse art forms that he thinks could facilitate his job.

Every form of folk literature in the world has its own distinctive features that differentiate it from other folk literatures. However, Kashmiri folk literature, is unique in the subcontinent for being the representative of a unique people who have a very long history of isolation from the rest of the world. The isolation is because of the insolation of the valley by insurmountable mountains from all sides and the perilous mountainous routes through passes that remain closed for most of the months every year. It is quite recently in history that the Valley has become accessible though the National Highway and air transport, reaching the valley in the past meant a month's long expedition through precarious mountain passes. The geographical isolation from mainland India by the physical barriers of the Pir Panjal and Nangaparbat Mountain ranges has resulted in the development of a folk literature that is drastically different from that of other parts of the subcontinent. Kashmiri folk literature, has developed many characteristics that are interesting in terms of their affinities with Central Asia and Iran. In spite of various cataclysmic changes, onslaughts, aggressions, this art has retained, nurtured and sustained many salient features that make its tradition immune to any radical transformation. All the folklorists and anthropologists are, therefore, deeply interested in its unique and traditional identity.

Besides being conservative in nature, Kashmiri Dastan is variegated. Kashmir has come into contact with many conquering peoples of other parts of the world like the Greeks, the Kushans, the Huns, the Iranians, the Chaks, the Mughals, the Afghans, the Sikhs and the Dogras. The physical contact with these peoples for considerable stretches of time have left an indelible imprint of their folk literature and enriched their narratives.

Besides imbibing themes, plots, characters, and narrative techniques of other languages, the art of Dastan goi has borrowed various performing arts as are helpful not only in supplementing the narration but also enhance the impact of the audience. Kashmiri Dastan goi has also retained many indigenous elements of performing arts that are used occasionally at relevant places by the experts in the art. Every element of performing art is subject to the emotive atmosphere of the narration, the event of presenting the Dastan and the availability of material tools available to the artist. Let us discuss various forms of performing arts that are considered integral parts of Kashmiri Dastan goi.

Daleela Gor (The Narrator)

Before the advent of modern means of entertainment the daleela gor occupied a respectable position in the society. It was essentially an hereditary occupation, but anyone could opt for it as his occupation. Generally it was a male profession as one had to be a roaming artist. In many eras the daleelagor was also called 'shair' or a folk poet.

Walter Lawrence wrote in his The Valley of Kashmir:

> The Shairs must be distinguished from the Bhaggats for they never act. They are either minstrels who sing to the accompaniment of a guitar, or the village poets, who suddenly spring up in the midst of business and recite in a loud and shrill tone the praises of the most influential person present. I knew many of these poets, and have spent many hours listening patiently to rhymes which seemed to have no end, and which jumbled up in a very curious manner oriental tropes with the most commonplace and technical terms of survey and revenue work. It is good to give these poets a few rupees, for they are often miserably poor. Many of whom I have met are unfortunately not quite sane, and one, a Muslim, who had formerly been a tutor to a high official, was hopelessly given to drinking, and justified his propensity by quotations from the Persian poets. He reviled me in the strongest language when I declined to give him whisky,

and said that the 'iron age; of the Hindus had indeed arrived, and left my camp in tears.[1]

The folk poets, or *shairs*, were seen almost in every nook and corner of the Valley up to the middle of the twentieth century. They appeared unexpectedly in the compound and sand tales of love, infidelity, wars, calamities, and transience of life. They could play on their rustic or *saarang*, which was a simple stringed instrument which produced poignant tunes by rubbing the bow on the strings made of the goat's gut. Usually two feet long, it consisted of a body carved from a single cedar wood with three hollow chambers: *yad* (tummy) *cheety* (chest) and *magaz* (brain). The *yad* is the resonance chamber and is covered by parchment made of goat skin. The bridge supported 35 sympathetic steel strings and three main gut strings that pass through it. The three gut strings are bowed with a heavy horse-hair bow and are beaten by nails. The neck made of bone or horns is the place where the player's fingers slide. The remaining 35 steel strings are sympathetic strings. A properly tuned s*arangi* creates melodious meowing, with tones played on any of the main strings eliciting echo-like resonance. The melodies of the sarangi always enhanced the nostalgia and poignancy of the *Dastan* narrated by the *shair*, referred to above. Most of the *Dastans* played on the sarangi used to be highly romantic and tragic in import. The artist as a performer of the sarangi usually remembered all the *Dastans* and the art of narration by heart as it was primarily an oral art. The artists learnt the tales from their *ustaads* or teachers and never deviated even in minute details. The rhyme scheme and the word repetitions helped their memory. Most of these wandering story-tellers were blind and used their walking stick to travel from one village to another. Some of them were, of course supported by their disciples, generally young boys of miserably poor families.

One of the most celebrated storytellers was Hatim Tilwony, son of Sabir Tilwony who lived at Panzal village in Lar *parganah* in the last decades of the nineteenth century. World famous orientalist Sir Aurel Stein, translator of *Rajatarangani*, came to Kashmir in 1894 and met Hatim Tilwony at a mountain resort Mahand Marg near Lar. Stein recorded many Dastans from the storyteller and with the help of a famous scholar, Govind Koul recorded the stories in Roman transliteration but also got them translated and analysed by George Abraham Grierson, into English. Writing about the astounding memory power of the folk-storyteller, he wrote about him in 1910 when he came to Kashmir again after fourteen years.

> Though wholly illiterate, he was able to recite them (the stories) all at any desired rate of speech which might suit our ears and pens; to articulate each word separate from the context, and to repeat it, if necessary, without any change in pronunciation. Nor did the order of his words or phrases ever vary after however long an interval he might be called upon to recite a certain passage again. The indication of two or three initial words repeated from my written record would be quite sufficient to set the disc moving in this living phonographic machine.

The collection of tales, or *Dastans* recorded and translated by Aurel Stein is a valuable source of information about the art of *daastangoi* in Kashmiri. It is a collection of 12 *Dastans,* which are an amalgam of verse and highly stylized prose. They show great variety in the use of various stylistic and narrative stratagems to enhance the impact of the *Dastans.* Let us discuss one such *daastan*, titled *Tota sunz Kath* (The Tale of a Parrot). The story starts with a typical traditional *Dastan* style:

> Dapaan ustad shahar ak gau shehri Iran. Tati os paadshah. Temy siy chhu naav Bahadur Khan, temy os kormut bag zanaanan kyt. Tot ees ni vath geerzaanas. Tethy baagas manz gav peedi fakierah. nazar baazav ker naza, khabardaarav niy khabar amyis paadshahas. Dopuk fakierah tsaav baagas manz. Buzun paadshahan. Hyotun seety wazier. Gayi that baagas manz, wuchhun atyi fakier. Lachhyi noo chiy har vatyi bina
>
> *Booz vafadar anqah,*
> *Ha fakiro yor kot tsakhoo*
> *Katyi ko chhukh katyi pyaThi aakho*
> *Fakier dapaan:*
> *Kor mya seelah, tuhund khyov mya kya,*
> *Booz vafadar anqah.*

Tr. This is what my Master told me:

There was a certain country, the land of Persia, and it was ruled by a king named Bahadur Khan. He made a garden for his womenfolk, into which no stranger was allowed to enter; but once there came into it a Faqir. The discerners then discerned him, and the newsmen gave the news to the King. They said, "A Faqir has come into the garden." The king heard, and took with him his Vizier. To the garden they went and there he saw the Faqir.

The Almighty, who hath a hundred thousand names, watcheth over every path.

Hark ye, loyalty is monstrous rare.

Where dost thou belong? Whence art thou come?"

Quoth the Faqir:

I came but for a stroll. What of yours have I eaten? Hark ye, loyalty is monstrous rare.[3]

The pithy sentences are very short, each with one finite verb. Many of the clichéd phrases of the Dastan are used like 'dapaan ustad… gov, end rhymes, traditional agents like Anqa (= Rara Avis, a mythological bird) Faqir with miraculous powers….etc. Then after the prelude in prose the Dastans go all of a sudden, as if in a frenzy, starts singing in accompaniment of his Sarangi.

This typical blending of narrating, singing and playing is common to all the 12 tales.

Some other performing arts that go into making of a typical daastan are: hikit, roh, gaaraayey, pachanagma, chakir, vanwun. Dameely, saang, and mime, and mask wearing.

Rof is a combination of song and dance. The word implies an ecstatic state of mind, and is introduced in the story-telling process when the emotions reach the crescendo. There was a time when even men-folk could participate in rof, but the form of dance is now exclusively a women's domain. It is a form of group song in which women, generally young girls, make two or three groups by concatenating their arms and sing such songs as are synchronised with their rhythmic backward and forward steps. When the song reaches its climax, the interlaced three groups gracefully move about in the available space and cross through one another. And then the most agile girls one by one perform individually while the others continue dancing and singing.

A rof is generally associated with the festivals of Eid and celebration of the birth of various saints, but since culture has become a part of the democratic institutions, rof is arranged for on every significant event, be it the Independence Day, the Republic Day or the annual day of an institution. Rof is now an integral part of composite cultural programmes that are arranged to forge and strengthen national integration and communal harmony. It is also an important segment of various charity shows and awareness programmes.

Hyikit is an optional element of rof. It is performed by two players who interlace their hands and bend their bodies in opposite directions to maintain a certain degree of pull and perform according to the rhythm of the song. The players in a romping manner revolve about a fixed point on the ground and continue to perform until one of the competitors gets tired or swoons by gyrating. The winner then gets a fresh challenger. The thrill and excitement are enhanced when the singers sing melodiously in keeping with the brisk rhythm of the dancers. The rotating locks of hair and the head-dresses add further charm to the dance.

Bachi Nagmi is a dance associated with group singing called chhakir. Young boys with kohl in their eyes and dressed as female dancers dance at the end of a full session of singing. The embellished attire, called peishwaza, and ankle-girdle of jingling bells, called rwonyihor, are reminiscent of an ancient dance form in which female dancers excelled. Besides dancing, the dancer, known as bachi-koT, displays various skills like carrying a burning lamp on his forehead, or rotating a winnowing pan in such a way that the burning lamp or a tumbler filled water placed on it does not fall. Bachinagma is still an integral part of marriages festivity. Bachanagma was used in the Dastangoi function as a part of festivity in the marriage halls and even the young boys and girls could accompany the batchikot who was considered neither male nor female. It was very rarely that erotic passion could mar the event when elders of the family objected to it.

Hafiz nagma is glorious legacy of Kashmiri culture. A Hafiza was a female singer and dancer who used to have a vast memory of Kashmiri mystical poetry. She sang with full orchestra either at her appointed place or at the houses of the aristocrats. She was not only an entertainer but an educator too. The tradition petered out with the end of feudalism and advent of modern culture. In 1845 G.T.Vigne wrote about the Hafizas of the time:

> The village of Changus, only a few miles from Achibul, was celebrated in times gone by as containing a colony of dancing girls, whose singing and dancing were more celebrated than those of any other part of the valley. I have heard Sumad Shah and other old men breathe forth sighs of regret, and expressions of admiration, when speaking of days that were past; and the grace and beauty of one of the Changus' danseuses, whose name was, I think Lyli, and long since dead, seemed to be quite fresh in their recollection.[4]

Tambuury-nagma

In olden days groups of singers of Sufi poetry and tales of romance and valour in verse wandered about in villages and towns to entertain people. The stringed percussion instrument that they used was called tambour and their singing was called tambuury-nagma. The artists following the art of narrating tales of romance and imagination along with playing on the tambour, were much like the artists who played the saarang, discussed already. Usually a solitary person could perform both functions, but sometimes two folk-artists did the job in collaboration, one narrating the story and the other playing the instrument.

Vyiegy natsun

A devotional form of female dance associated with the customs of meikhal, that is the investiture of male child with yoonyi the sacred thread, is known as Vyiegy natsun. The boy is seated on the picture (vyuug) drawn with turmeric on the ground and then all the women and girls of the family dance around it. Similarly when the bride and bridegroom are seated on the vyuug, the females of the family perform vyiegy natsun.

Bandi natsun is a dance that is incorporated in a theatrical performance of banndi paethir, the most popular form of Kashmiri folk theatre. It is a vibrant dance on high-pitch music of dhool and shahnai and any other improvised musical instrument. The highly embellished and stylised outfit and mask dances are some permanent features of a typical baandi natsun.

Dameely, being associated with devotion, is thus a form of Kashmiri folk dance that has still its professional practitioners. It is said that Dameely is one of the significant forms of folk dance of Kashmir. Unfortunately it is now a forgotten legacy of the past.

We are near Swoybug village of Badgam, the centre of Dameely dancers.

Dameely is one of the oldest forms of Kashmiri folk dance, now on the verge of extinction. There are still some practising folk artists who keep this dance form alive. Like other forms of folk dances of Kashmir, Dameely too is fast vanishing from people's memory. Some other folk forms of Kashmiri dance are:

> Dameely is a male dance form in which thirty to forty men, young as well as old, participate. The dance is euphoric in nature and does not follow any prescribed pattern. The dancers may improvise according to the situation.

It is essentially a congregational performing art. It does not follow traditional distinction between the dancer of the proscenium, stage and the audience. Being participatory in nature, the audiences too can participate in it.

A typical Dameely performance has three components: dance, instrumental music and masquerade.

The instruments used in a Dameely are: seven drums, a few shahnai-type wind instrument called swarnay and daphs. In addition to these instruments the performers may create rhythm with the help of the wands that they carry in their hands.

The rhythm is accentuated further by the taps of the brisk steps.

The rhythm of the drums and swarnay is of four types, each type named by the professionals: Sweery, ruush, charkha, and dakhli. To start the dance, the wind instruments swarnay play the following melody:

tah…tah…tah…taa (three times)
sah… sah… sah…saa (4 times)

The swarnay symphony is then accompanied by the rhythm of the drums in loud pitch. The rhythm has the following patterns:

din-din-taka-din-taka-din-taka
din-din-taka-din-taka-din-taka-din-din-taka

When the rhythm reaches its crescendo, all the dancers start whirling with the rhythm of the instruments. This is called damaali sweery. The rhythm has the following order:

din-taka-din… din-taka-din…taka-din-taka
din-taka-din…taka-din-taka-din-taka

This is done nine times.

When the number of the audiences reaches the satisfaction of the performers, they play other parts of the dance. They intermittently pray for the well-being of the community and the cheerful audiences utter "amen!"

This is followed by a long interlude of invocation to God, and the saints. They dance keeping their hands raised. The audiences grow solemn and they too raise their hands to the sky. The good-auguring prayers are like these:

Yaa Allah yemyi alaqi kyan lukan kar yeeryiy
O God ! bless the people of this are.

Yaa Allah yemyi kul keshyiryi hindyan lukan kar yeeryiy
O God ! bless all the inhabitants of Kashmir.

Yaa Allah yemyi kul aalmikyan lukan kar yeeryiy
O God ! Bring plenty and good health to all people of the world.

Yaa Allah! Zindan dyi or zuv ti dor koth
O God ! Keep all the living healthy.

Yaa Allah! Yemyi aalmi gemytyan kar magfirat
O God ! Absolve all those who have left this world.

Yaa Allah! bemaaran kar shafaa
O God! Restore good health to the ailing.

Yaa Allah! kooryi vaalyan soz khriedar
O God ! Send suitable matches to parents of daughters.

Yaa Allah! beroozgaaran dyi roozgaar
O God ! Provide jobs to the jobless.

Yaa Allah! faslas kar barkat
O God ! Make our harvest plentiful.

Yaa Allah! seeny gwanah kar maaf.....
O God ! Pardon all our sins.

The interlude for prayers is followed by dance and music again. The drums play *syataal* (three-note music) and the dance is the three-step dance.

The crescendo of the drums is followed by the beating of the *daph*.

The performers start showing their individual feats.

Each of them dances till he can hold his breath back. The spectators cheer them in admiration.

The dancers swing their heads vigorously while uttering mystical words with the rhythm of the instruments. This ecstatic phase of the dance is called *zikir*. Sometimes the performer of *zikir* falls in trance and the spectators hold him in their arms.

The *daph* concert is immediately followed by a performance of the dance form called *gatkibeeziy*. It is a crude form of some old marshal art. The word *gatkibeeziy* is a compound word: *gaatak+beeziy* which means feat of fatal attacks. The dancers carrying swords in their hands attack each other is the swirl jumping dance.

The *dameely* performers again pray for the good of all.

The spectators reward them in cash or kind like rice, bread, clothes, etc.

The performers gather the bonus and disperse.

Bonus, however, is not the incentive of the *dameely* dance. It has a ritualistic and communitarian purpose. It is performed during various festival at various shrines. The performers of the *dameely* have been ordained by their forefathers to perform only to pay homage to the revered saints, commemorate the dead, and pray for abundance and prosperity. It is also a collective thanksgiving for a plentiful harvest.

The spectators respect the *dameely* performers as it is integrated with their beliefs.

People believe that any form of disrespect or indifference to the *dameely* performs can portend evil or harm.

The origin of *dameely* is not known. Keeping in view its antiquity, it can be surmised that it is a continuation of Buddhist ritual called *dhammam-gatya* in which teachers danced while reciting teachings of Lord Buddha and fables to the novices.

The art of *dameely* has some parallels in other parts of North India and in Pakistan. The ritualistic art, called *dhamaal* of Gujarat is an instance in which male members of the Siddi community perform it with weird costumes. It is said that this dance came from Africa.

However, folklorists and anthropologists are of the opinion that dance and drum beating around fixed poles, trees and bonfires is a widespread ritual in almost every part of the world. Its purpose is to invoke deities to bring plentiful harvests, propitiate souls of saints and heroes and to exorcise bad spirits, and to stop spread of diseases.

Dameely is an integral part of festivity at various shrines of Kashmir.

Some of the important shrines where *dameely* is performed are:

1. Shrine of Baba Nasib-ud Din Ghazi at Bijbihara
2. Shrine of Baba Janbaaz Wali at Baramullah
3. Shrine of Lala Baba Sahib at Zakoorah
4. Shrine of Baba Shakoor-ud Din at Zainagir
5. Shrine of Khani Meely Seeb near Tsari Sharief

The festival at the shrine of Baba Nasib-ud Din Ghazi in May-June is the principal centre event of dameely activity. The shrine is in honour of a venerated saint. It is situated at Bijbihara on the National High Way. The professionals belonging to various *dameely* clans living in various parts of the valley throng together. Carrying their colourful standards (*alam*) on poles, they usually come walking from distant villages, particularly Zolav-Wahthore of Badgam district.

They perform in various villages during their journey. The purpose is to make the rural devotees know that the date of the festival is approaching.

The artists begin performing a few days ahead of the festival. They dance to the music in the inner compound of the shrine. The purpose is to herald the festival.

The festival lasts for three days. Rural folks watch the dance as a part of paying homage to the saint and also to seek the blessings of the *dameely* artists, called *Damaali Faquir*.

People believe that the dance and music can bring good harvests, obviate calamities, and cure diseases.

The use of awful masks by the *Damaali Faquir*s is to avert fear, and misfortune. Fond mothers, therefore, hand over their children to the *faquir*s so that they are made immune to fear and disease.

The festival at the shrine at Zakoora near Srinagar is only one of its kind. Professional *dameeli Faquirs* are not found uniformly in Kashmiri society; they are a distinct social class and live at various specific villages. A few villages that were once famous for *dameeli Faquirs* are: Swaayibug, Zwalav-Wahthore, Kelyshah Saeb (near Kulgam) Akingaam near Anantnag

After a festival is over, the artists have to wait for the next festival.

They have a calendar of all the festivals in the Valley. They talk of the olden ages when their art was much admired and the apathy of the people of modern times. They tidy their contraption and outfits and keep them ready for the next event.

Dameeli Faquirs pursue other occupations to seek their livelihood because *dameely* is associated with specific festivals on specific dates. They work as roaming singers like Ladishah and Gaaraayey, exorcising evil spirits, working as middlemen in marriages, and curers of bone ailments.

There was a time, just fifty years ago, when *dameely* was a full-time occupation for its practitioners.

Dameely dance was also arranged by the aristocrats on various significant occasions like marriages, ceremony of entering a newly constructed house *gharpravesh,* worship of arsenal called *astar puuza*, and ablution ceremonies.

Radical transformation in economic conditions resulted in major changes in the social and cultural structure of Kashmiri society. The *dameely* artists have other profitable occupations like growing apple orchards, cultivation of paddy and doing government jobs.

Those who still pursue it as their main profession, live in dismal poverty.

Since social and cultural transformations are irreversible, we cannot hope to revive the feudal cultural milieu in which roaming entertainers like *dameely* artists had a significant role. However, the government and various NGOs can definitely preserve this rich legacy of ancient times. Paying the artists a handsome remuneration, making it an integral part of cultural tourism and improving its techniques, costumes, music and other accoutrements, can save it from the all-swaying onslaught of fast changing electronic audio-visual means of entertainment.

Gaarayey

An old form of *Dastangoi* was pursued by group-performers who were called gaaraayey. The word Garaayey, though etymologically very intriguing, is in fact a singing utterance of two Kashmiri words *gari* (house) and *aayay* (have come). The performers of this art form were generally eunuchs who lived in closed in-groups in various villages, but hardly any commoner knew about their dwelling. The most surprising aspect of them is that they had a very intricate and effective network throughout the valley and wherever there was any event of child-birth or marriage in any village, even far-flung hamlets, they sprang up as if from nowhere. All the members of the group, except one dancing boy, used to be attired in snow-white attire. The dancing boy wore a long cascading bell-shaped and embroidered outer-garment embellished with small coloured pieces of glass, and jingle bells. The party appeared in the compound of the house whose joy of wedding or child-birth was still fresh. They started with a song that bore the rhyme "gaaraayay" (We have come to your house.) The accoutrement of the gaaraayay-singers were drums of various sizes, a *swarnay* (reed-flute) and metal plates or cymbals. When the required tempo of music was attained, they sang the repetitive line while the chief singer sang of some event of bygone times, like Yousuf Zulaikha, Sheereen Khusrav, Laila wa Majnoon, or Akanandun. They would sing only when the members of the house came out and made a ring around them and the neighbours also joined them.

Mask-dance

The mask-dance, that is playing the roles of animals, supernatural beings, fairies, demons, good-auguring agents and bad-auguring agents, the kings and queens, is as old as Kashmiri culture. The mask-dance was in fact a medium of conveying a massage to the audience through a story that involved mythical characters as well as historical ones. The audience appreciated when they were conscious that it was an art-form not a slice of reality, but at the same time appreciated the degree of verisimilitude in the performance of the human actors wearing masks.

CHAPTER 4

Important *Dastans* and Use of Drama in Them

Kashmir has been both a meeting place and watershed of numerous tales of fantasy and imagination. There are hundreds of tales, called *luki-kathi* (folk-tales) that have been handed over from one generation to the next by countless unknown story-tellers and eventually have reached our present times. Being the most popular form and method of folk-recreation, even the common people without any special prowess could have a role in the transfer of the memory-based literature from one age to the next. They often did not need any professional master of story-telling to beguile them in the harsh wintry nights when heavy snow made any other activity of life almost impossible. The members of a family, usually big, including uncles, aunts, cousins and other kin, would assemble in a cosy room and any of the elderly members could make others, usually children, make imaginative soaring in the world of fantasy. Since almost all the tales were already known, and belonged to a common shared memory, it was the art of narration that mattered. It would rarely happen that anyone made any change, addition or alteration in the stock pile of stories and *daastan*s. The sequence of events continued almost automatically without any premeditative thought; the listeners curiously took interest in how the teller roped in the incidents towards a pre-determined end. The narrator, in order to make the narration-listening process more lively, would frequently ask questions like: "Do you know what happened then?" Do you hear me?" The attentive listener would surely look forward to the next event. Thus we see that *Dastan Goi*, although a distinct art with its definite characteristics, was mostly a shared and communal art.

The repertoire of *Dastan*s in the Kashmiri language is very vast as it has imbibed numerous tales from all those nations and linguistic communities which during the course of times, for various social, political, religious and cultural reasons came into contact, direct as well a s indirect, with the people of Kashmir. It is, therefore amazing that many of the *Dastan* in the language, consists of characters, visual details, fauna and flora, and background of distant lands like Africa, Arab, or Central Asia. It is a universal feature of the *Dastan* that the more displaced it is from the mundane and the commonplace, the more fascinating it is. It also enhances the probability of the improbable or makes even impossible probable. Thus it is interesting to note that we have Abyssinan, Chinese, Iranian, Turkamenian, characters, animals, and cultural elements in our *Dastans* are much admired by the rustic people without any element of question or cynicism. It is the general force of the *Dastan* that creates 'suspension of disbelief' and makes the tale of imagination interesting. Let us analyse some of the most popular *Dastans* In Kashmiri and see how the professional *Dastan* narrator uses his individual talent to keep the tradition living.

About Dastan H.B Pasoy wrote:

> *Dastan* is ornate oral history, common among the peoples of Central Asia. It conveys the revered and cherished value systems from one generation to the next over millennia. It is part of the permanent record of a people or a confederation. It lives on as a unifying charter in the consciousness of the people whose lives and exploits gave birth to it. It is the national anthem, birth certificate and literary heritage of its owners. It provides the framework to bond a coherent *oymak*, the ancestral unit, a division of a greater confederation. Members of the *oymak* share one language, religion and history.
>
> The influence and authority of the Dastan – as well as the reverence in which it is held – are shown by Yesevi's quotation above. Even an influential Sufi leader such as Ahmet Yesevi (from the city of Yese in Central Asia) saw the need to elevate his teachings to the level of a Dastan. This reference by Yesevi points to the established tradition of keeping alive and disseminating important information through Dastans. The Dastan has also been used at various times to propagate religious ideas or doctrines, although the genre in its original form is not religious.
>
> In the Altai region, the tradition of "expression and celebration of ancestral exploits and identity" first appears in a series of stelea. Apparently the earlier Altaians did not have a need to affix a label to the genre. In the early eighth century, the ruler Bilge Kagan in the Kul Tegin stelas states: "*Bu sabimin adguti asid, qatigdi tinla*" ("Hear these words of mine well, and listen hard!"). Some three hundred years later, Kashgarli Mahmut, in his *Diwan Lugat at-Turk* (1070s) uses the word saw *(sab, sav)* to indicate proverbs, messages and admonitions handed down by wise men. About a century after Kashgarli Mahmut, Ahmet Yesevi (d. 1167) wrote: "Let the scholars hear my wisdom/ Treating my word as a *Dastan*, attain

> their desires." This is the earliest recorded mention so far found to refer to the label Dastan in Central Asia.
>
> The prevailing designations in the Altai, such as *jir* (as in *batirlik jiri*) and *chorchok* suggest that the genre may have been called *dastan* further to the West. The contents, format and intent have remained essentially the same. The *dastan*, in most cases, is named for the alp (or *batir*), the central figure or hero, who may be male or female, e.g. Oghuz Khan, Manas, Koroglu, Kirk Kiz. At other times, the term *batir* or alp is appended to the name: Kambar Batir, Chora Batir, Alp Er Tunga and Alpamysh.
>
> Over a period of millennia the neighbouring Altaic/Turk, Indian and Persian literary genres in Central Asia came into contact and may have influenced each other. Since the study of these genres is by and large in their infancy, it is too early to venture authoritative opinions on these aspects.

Dastans commemorate the deeds of fearless and capable men and women. They rise from among the people when critically important tasks need to be performed. Often this task is to fight for the independence of a polity, or group of polities which we now refer to as confederation. The exploits of these battle-tested alps on behalf of their people are celebrated and immortalised by reciters known as the *ozan* (some of whom composed *Dastans*). Almost always the *ozan* (sometimes known as b*ahshi, kam* or shaman) will accompany himself with a musical instrument known as *kopuz*.

Like any other country of the Central Asia Kashmir too, with a long history of oral literature has been the fountainhead of numerous tales. The Dastans of Kashmir have worked as a strong cohesive force that maintained the identity of the people by acting as a medium of transference of moral and spiritual values and at the same time providing the people with an inexhaustible source of entertainment. The *Dastan*s, numerous as well as various, are both indigenous and adapted from other languages through cultural contact, however, the distinction is not much sharp because the adapted dastans too have undergone many structural changes in terms of characters, setting, and moral and aesthetic values. The *Dastan* of *Hiemaal and Neegyraay* is certainly a native tale, but it has many parallels in world folk literature because all the incidents, characters and objects are symbolic in import that are essentially secular and universal.

Hiemaal – Neegyraay

It was a scorching summer day and Balavir, a simple hardworking Brahmin of a village, named Balapur, was having a sweet midday siesta under a dense pine tree. He lived a miserable life as his wife, without a male issue, always tortured him by her continuous nagging. While he slept, a long and beautiful snake emerged from some hole under the huge boulders that lay all around the place. The snake calmly crept into its luggage that he was holding as a pillow under his head. The effect of the serenity of the pine shade was such as made him keep sleeping until it was almost evening. He woke up and walked fast to his home. He was lucky that his wife, along with his daughter, Hiemal, in her early teens, had gone to the spring to fetch water. He kept his luggage in the kitchen as it contained all flour, salt, and some spices that would last them for a few days. In order to avoid his wife's abuses he went to his kitchen garden to pick some vegetables to cook. He deliberately spent longer time in the kitchen garden than was needed.

He descended behind the mountains, and he, with a bunch of turnips and greens in his hands returned to his home. Before entering his hut, he held his ear to the wooden door, to hear if his wife was in a good mood. He was amazed to hear big laughter of his wife, his daughter and some strange male fellow. Being curious he peeped through a rent in the mud-wall of his house. What he saw inside was nothing less than a shock to him. An exceedingly handsome young man attired in royal clothes was on a wooden basket that he had taken for a seat. Some precious fruits and shining gems were placed in clay plates. Hiemal, propped against a wooden pillar, cherished eating an apple while his wife sitting in front of the princely person was keenly attentive to what the stranger said. What he heard through the rent, was not easy for him to understand. The strangers told her that his name was Nagraay and that he was a snake by nature. He told them that he was the king of the nether world, called Talpataal.. He dallied away from his palace as he wanted to have some fresh air of the terrestrial world because his wives had made life miserable for him. He told them how he sneaked into Balaram's luggage to reach their house. He beseeched them for asylum. On hearing this Balaram, in his ecstasy entered his hut and embraced Naegyraay. Nagraay thus became a member, just like a son, of Balavir's small family.

One day when Balavir and his wife, the two lived a happy life and quarrel-free life, returned from their corn field. On entering their hut they found their pretty daughter Hiemal shedding tears and asking Nagray to marry her. Neegyraay tells them that he already has several wives, and cannot do so. After much persuasion, he agrees to the proposal and decides to stay in Balvir's house. He gives up his royal glamour and lives the life of a simple villager and helps the family in doing many odd jobs of agriculture.

The village girls are jealous of Heemal for having got such a handsome and healthy groom and worked ceaselessly to make the family do well. One of the girls, once watches him having a bath in a spring under the dense willow trees. She is amazed to see the snake like feature of his body. She comes running to her friend Heemal and tells her the secret. Heemal is not ready to believe what she says.

One day while Neegyraay was tilling the field of his father-in-law, he sees a potter's wife carrying a huge basket full of earthen vessels on her head. She is actually one of the spouses of Naagray who lives with her kith and kin in the nether –world. She recognises her husband and goes to Heema'ls house and tells her that Naagraay is not a human being but the king of serpents. When Nagraay is home in the evening, Heemal asks her to show her his real nature. In spite of Naagraay's much dithering, she is adamant in her urge to see him in his real form. She arranges for a huge pot full of milk and keeps near Naagraay. She insists that he should step into the cauldron filled with milk. Naagraay, having no choice, plunges into the cauldron of milk. He disappears and reaches down to the Nether World of serpents; Heemal is left wailing for her serpent lover. She wanders all around, from village to village to find him but there is no trace of Naagraay. One day she meets a Faquir and reveals her woes to him. The Faqir by his spiritual power, helps her reach the Nether World, and meet Naagraay. Naagraay, seeing his earthly human beloved, is thrilled and asks her to stay in her palace as a nurse.

One day, it happens that Naagraay's small children, who are actually small snakes, drink hot rice water that Heemal has left unattended in the house. The kids' throats want to drink hot rice gravy. Their mother in her wrath stings her and Heemal falls unconscious. She takes her to her native village and keeps her in the thicket of willows. After some days, Heemal recovers from her unconscious state, and finds herself back to her native home. She haggardly loiters from village to village and, is finally wed to a rich merchant.

Naagraay, being mad in his desire for Heemal, re-emerges from his Nether world and roams in the villages of Kashmir. He finally finds her but is dejected to see her wed to a merchant. While he narrates his tale of sorrow to his beloved, the merchant enters. Seeing a huge snake in front of Heemal, he is angry and kills the snake (Naagraay) and dismembers his body. Heemal cries in her lament and decides to renounce the world. She takes the pieces of he demon lover in a sheet of cloth, carries them to her paternal house at Balapore and arranges for a pyre for the cremation of her dead lover. When the flames rage high she all of a sudden jumps into the pyre and commits self-cremation (sati). Since self-cremation is a sin, the two lovers re-appear on the surface of the earth but in the form of two springs, which are still near Rimbara, always giving out fresh and cold water.

There are several interpretations of the legend, but the legend is, before being an allegory, an immortal *Dastan*. There are many incidents that are replete with dramatic action and as such the Dastan has been presented on the stage.

Akanandun

One of the most haunting tales of fantasy, imagination and magic, rife with mystical interpretations is the *Dastan* of *Akanandun*; it is certainly one of the oldest *Dastans* in the language. The basic theme, social setting, mythical background, and belief in transfer of soul through magic – all intimate a very old archetype that man's affirmation lies in annihilation, or the reward of self-annihilation is the affirmation of the self.

The very title suggests that Akanandun (The One Beautiful) suggests that the *Dastan* needs reflective study and not to be taken at its surface level. Without going into the intellectual intricacies of the elements of the *Dastan* let us see how the element of drama gets unfolded at every stage of the narrative.

The *Dastan* begins with the following dramatic enunciation.

A Brahmin and his consort are sitting morosely in the living room of their shanty, each absorbed in their daily chores. The wife is spinning at her spinning wheel and the Brahmin is intertwining the spun wool threads on his rotating hand-wheel. The Brahmin croons some old lay to himself and occasionally looks at the fading face of his wife. The wife heaves a deep sigh. In order to beguile her, the Brahmin sings aloud a mystic line.

A loud thud is heard, suggesting that somebody slams the outer door of the compound rather carelessly. The couple start and look at each other with grim eyes. In the meantime they hear the someone calling the Brahmin's name a little discourteously.

Stranger: Hey Rama Tsandra! What are you doing sitting idle in your cell? Come out and see spring is in full bloom. Winter has ended. Come out and give up your sloth… I am your old Jogi at your door. I am hungry. Get me a little bread and sauce. (Inside the house)

Rama Tsander: (With aghast eyes) Oh It is Sadanand Jogi. I had forgotten that he had promised me last year that he would revisit us hear. What a careless fellow I am. You get up and cook something for Sadanand.

Bahat: Yes, yes. I remember. He had given us some promise that something good is to happen to us.

{Rama Tsander gets up with some effort and stretches his body, and then unlatches the wooden door, The door opens with a long squeak. Sadanand enters, holding his bowl in his hand and a bag tied to the long stick that he carries on his shoulder. He laughs aloud and without seeking permission enters. Bahat gets a mat and stretches it for him to sit. Sadanand squats and croons some cryptic words.}

Sadanand: Tell me why do you look so withered? Is there something that still ails you? Bhagwan has given you a lot of crops, sheep and hens. Yet you look so sad and depressed. Why?

Bahat: Oh God's friend, Jogi you know all, yet you lacerate us by these question.

Ramatsandar: Now we are getting old. True God has been very kind to us, but…

Bahat: O God's friend! Tell us what should we offer you ? We owe all our joys to you. You gave us the reason to keep living. Should we get almond milk? We have also a warm blanket of finest fleece for you? Tell us what more do you want.

Sadanand: Do not try to prevaricate. You know what we want. Remember your promise.

Bahat: O Jogi ! You know all the secrets of life. I hope you have mercy on us. You gave us Akanandun. He is the only hope that sustains us in this old age.

Sadanand: (Furiosly) I say remember the promise. Where is Akanandun? He is needed by God the Merciful.

Ramachander: Yes we have firm faith in God's mercy. God cannot be cruel to us. If you want him back, then please snatch away this fragile life from us. Why should we be an unwanted burden on this earth? You kill us then you may take our son back. We have nurtured him with our blood.

Sadanand: Where is Akanandun? I need my Akanandun back. He was trusted with you. Mind, today he is twelve years old. Today is the day of his going back to God's abode from where he came.

(The old couple start crying and beating their breasts in wailing.)

Yes today is the end of the deed. I shall send him back. Call him now. Don't cry for nothing. Nothing shall avail you nothing. (Calls aloud) Akanandun! Hey Akanandun! Come anon, lest it should be late.

Ramachander: He is at his school. …You know he is the pride of the school. He is so good in his studies. He has read many of God's scriptures. The teachers say that he is God's friend.

Sadanand: True, He is God's friend that is why he is back at God's abode. …No matter, I shall keep waiting. But stop crying. Don't annoy me.

(The terrified couple nestle close to each other. They stop crying, but they sob intermittently. Sadanand nonchalantly plays at his harp. The old couple, in horror, look askance at him.)

Sadanand: Get me some almond milk.

(Bahat half-heartedly gets up and walks towards the cooking place…. Sadanand continues playing his harp. He plays a melancholic note…. Bahat gets him a cup of hot almond-milk. Sadanand smilingly receives it and starts taking long sips. In the meantime, Akanandun enters frolicking. He is surprised to see the stranger in his house. Bahat holds him to her bosom. Ramachander goes near him and kisses his child.

Sadanand: Do not disturb him. Do not show this foolish parental fondness. I am not one to get moved to see you…. Akanandun! Come here you are my child.

(Akanandun joyously goes near the Jogi and sits in his lap.)

Akanandun: Are you a Jogi? You know all?

Sadanand: Of course I know all, my naughty child.

Akanandun: Then tell me the meaning of Trika.

Sadanand: Do not try my knowledge. I am after all a Jogi. I am not one be tested by a wanton child. Don't you make me angry… You know today is your last day in this house…

Akanandun: What do you mean?

Like the scene given above the whole action of the Dastan of Akanandun could be presented on the stage quite effectively and efficiently. The following sequence of five events is generally the preferred sequence:

- The Jogi visits the Brahman's house and gives them the boon of having a beautiful son.
- Akanandun is seen in his early childhood. Goes to the school is under the vigil of the Jogi. The child is the soul of his parents and his sisters.
- The child at the age of twelve is demanded back by the Jogi. Mourning in the house. Yet the parents acquiesce in the promised surrender.
- The Jogi slays the child, dismembers his body, cooks the flesh in a cauldron and then offers the cooked flesh to the parents.
- The child is summoned back. All are happy. The child, named Akanandun, is blessed to have a long and prosperous life, while being kind to all.

Human sacrifice is perhaps the most awful of all the totems. Though there is no evidence of human sacrifice in Kashmir and Central Asia, but there are certain folktales in which killing ones own dearest son for the joy of a Yogi or Pir is a recurring universal theme. In Kashmir the Story of *Akanandun* is one such story that has remained one of the most popular stories ever heard. Though it will be a travesty of the story to give it in summary as it is its structure of the narrative that is the secret of the charm of the story, yet it is worthwhile here.

There lived an old Brahman couple in a remote village of Kashmir. They had everything but lived a miserable life as they did not have a son. They performed all rituals to please their God to get a male issue, but all proved futile.

One day a Yogi with queer brightness in his eyes and in a negligee entered their house and asked for alms. The husband and wife gave the Yogi alms to his full satisfaction. The Yogi was happy with them and asked them why they looked so sad. They revealed the cause of their suffering to the Yogi.

The Yogi closed his eyes for a while and then opened his eyes. He laughed boisterously. "Why do you laugh? Tell us the secret O pitiless Yogi." The old Brahmin asked the Yogi.

"You are destined to have a son, but there is one condition," the Yogi told them.

"Yes, we are ready to fulfil all conditions however difficult and painful it might be."

"You shall have a son as pretty as the sun. Your life shall be filled with joy. He shall bloom into his teens, but then…" The Yogi stopped and began to pant.

"Then what?" asked the old couple with pallor on their wrinkled faces. "Tell us what is going to happen next?"

"You shall have to kill your own son and offer his flesh to me. Now tell me are you ready?"

The old couple shed tears and could not utter a word in reply.

"Tell me will you still yearn for the son?"

"Yes, yes O heartless Yogi, we are ready. Let us have the bliss of a son of our own."

"You shall have a son pretty as the sun," saying this the Yogi vanished into thin airs.

After nine months the wife of the Brahmin gave birth to a son as pretty as the sun. The child was named Akanandun. The house of the old couple was filled with joy. The father, the mother and their daughters nursed the child with all possible care. So absorbed were they in their glee that they did not even remember the Yogi's condition. Year after year passed till the boy was twelve.

One sunny afternoon when Akanandun was in his school, the Yogi with the same awesome brightness in his eyes and ruffled hair and in a negligee appeared in their house. The old couple shivered with fear. They sent one of their daughters to the school to keep Akanandun engaged in play so that the Yogi did not see him.

"Where is Akanandun, my child? I am feeling hungry."

This made the old couple cry loudly as if they wailed. But the Yogi was not moved, he guffawed in his usual way.

"O heartless Yogi, have pity on us. Do not snatch away our life from us. We shall offer you all dainties to quell your hunger, but spare the life of our son."

All screaming and wailing had no effect on the laughing Yogi.

Then with heavy hearts Akanandun was brought home. The Yogi's face brightened to see the child. He caressed the child and then asked his parents to get him a knife. The agonised parents got him the knife. The Yogi killed the boy, dismembered his body and cut all parts into smaller pieces. He put all the flesh into a pot and began to cook it.

When the flesh of the child was toughly cooked, the Yogi put it in plates, one for each inmate of the house. The father and mother watched him doing all this eyes aghast with horror. On the goading of the Yogi, they took their plates in their hands. There was still a plate full of the cooked flesh and there was no other person to have it. "Who is the other person to have that extra plate ?

"Akanandun, who else?" the Yogi said.

The bereaved couple wailed loudly to hear the Yogi's reply.

"Yes, it is for Akanandun, my dearest child. Call him in." The Yogi did not show any compassion.

"I say call Akanandun. He shall partake of this delicious food," the Yogi said sternly.

"Akanandun, my soul, where are you? Come on in. The yogi wants you." The mother called her son loudly but in a mournful voice.

Akanandun anon romped in, as bright as usual. The bereaved couple knew no bounds with joy to see their son unharmed. All were taken aback to see him there. They hugged him one by one and then looked towards the Yogi. He had disappeared again into thin air.

The boy Akanandun grew into a handsome young man and made his parents and other kindred happy. [9]

This story descended down to us from the remote past is reminiscent of the Aryans among whom human sacrifice prevailed. It has many parallels in Central Asian folklore and in Islamic history. The sacrifice stands for man's complete surrender before God's will and vanquishing desire and greed.

There are many tales of infidelity of women, and are narrated with the man's point of view. Being full of humour, folks like them for various tricks to conceal cuckoldry of men and their credulous naivety. The merchants who keep roaming from place to place are seen in various extramarital relations while they are themselves cuckolded for being away from home.

The merchants in the folklore of the region were roaming people who used to buy merchandise like ornaments, condiments, medicines, utensils, clothes, etc., from the town and then sold it to the rustic folk and the nomads. Called soodaagaar in the folklore, they are depicted as fraudulent people who used different kinds of dupes to entice the women and children and thus swindle them. They accepted money as well as rice, maize, wheat in bargain. There are many folk tales of the region in which the soodaagaar is shown as beaus also for whom the country damsels had strong fascination because they used to wander from village to village and the girls on the contrary were confined to their homes. Since the *Sodaagaars* remained out of their homes most of the time, they were deceived by their wives during their absence. There are many tales in which the soodaagaars are cuckolded by their wives and they never come to know about their wives infidelity. Many such tales about soodaagaars in Kashmiri have come from Central Asia through education in Persian texts like Gulistan and Bostan of Shaikh Saidi and the works of Farid-ud Din Attar. One of such tales is about a stupid merchant whose infidel wife uses different tricks to make his stupid husband believe that his wife is quite faithful. Here is a story that has come from the Persian sources.

The Stupid Merchant

A merchant who suspected the fidelity of his wife kept a talking parrot to spy on her while he was on his usual errands. He taught the parent to say what the weather was like when the paramour of his wife visited her in his absence.

The clever wife knew it.

While she enjoyed a night with her paramour, she produced artificial wind in the bed chamber and cast strong lights on the parrot's eyes. She also sprinkled a shower over the parrot.

When the merchant returned and asked the parrot about the weather, the parrot told him that there was a violent storm, thunders and lightning when the paramour visited his wife.

The merchant was convinced that the parrot lied and his wife was innocent.

Tale of a Parrot

This is what my Master told me:

> There was a certain country, the land of Persia, and it was ruled by a king named Bahadur Khan. He had many a garden for his womenfolk, into which no stranger was allowed to enter; but once there came into it a Faqir. The discerners the discerns then discerned him, and the newsmen gave the news to the King. Said they, "A Faqir has come into the garden.

> The King heard, and took with him his Vizir. To the garden they went, and there he saw the Faqir.

"O Faqir, how didst thou enter? Where dost thou belong? Whence art thou com?"

Quoth the Faqir:

I came but for a stroll. What of yours have I eaten?

Hark ye, loyalty is monstrous rare

It chanced that before the king there was a flowering plant, and at its foot a dead nightingale. As soon as they spoke angrily to the Faqir, he fell flat, lifeless to the ground, and as he did so the nightingale arose alive. Such magic power did he show the king. The nightingale flew out of the garden, and returned. Then it fell dead and the Faqir again became alive. He began to depart, but they entreated him saying:

> O Faqir, let me be thy servant!
>
> Cups of the cream of milk will I fill for thee.
>
> Special pilaos and dainties wilt thou not eat?
>
> Hark ye, loyalty is monstrous rare.

So the Faqir confided the secret of his magic power to the King, and the King confided it to his Vizir.

The King gave instructions to the Vizir, and he thus became proficient in the secret.

They went out hunting together.

Hark ye, loyalty is monstrous rare.

In the forest they saw a parrot dead,

"O vizir, how beautiful this must have been.

Put thou, I beseech thee, thy life into it but for a moment."

Hark ye, loyalty is monstrous rare.

Said the Vizir:-

"My King, for long hath it been dead.

A stink cometh from it; who knoweth when it died?

Hark ye, loyalty is monstrous rare.

For this did the King make urgent entreaty to the Vizir. "Fain would I see how beautiful the parrot was," but the Vizir refused to listen to him.

And, further, my master told me:-

In his heart there was treachery. At length the King himself abandoned his own body and entered into the parrot. Up rose the parrot, and flew about. Then the Vizir did a deed: he himself entered into the King's body. What was what had all along been in his heart.

The burden which had been the King's to bear,

That became laid upon the foolish Vizir.

Treachery was watching in him like a petitioner.

Hark ye, loyalty is monstrous rare.

The parrot is flying in the air, and the Vizir is in the body of the King. He stood up.

He mounted the King's horse and went into the army. He sad to them:

"The Vizir fell from his horse and is dead.

That was the news that the newsman brought.

Hark ye, loyalty is monstrous rare.

When this Vizir had done the deed, and when he had entered the King's body, in his hand had he raised his sword, and into small pieces did he cut his own dead body. Then said he to his army. "Go forth, ye archers, and ye gunmen. Whoever of you killeth a parrot, to him will given a reward. "When the parrot heard this order, he fled afar, and went to the Faqir, who on that day had been in his garden.

He gave the order to the archers.

"Pay ye heed, I pray, to my coaxing."

He gave an order that the parrot should be killed.

Hark ye, loyalty is monstrous rare.

Now, as for the real king, he was in the parrot, and had taken refuge with the Fair; so that parrot was not killed by anyone. One day the Vir-King sallied forth to hunt; and when he had reached a certain place he decried a hind. After it they made pursuit. They brought it into the army, and he said to them. "I will cut off the head of him who letteth her escape.

And, further, my Master told me:-

But the hind gave a sudden spring and leaped over the head of the Vizir-king himself. They pursued her Now the parrot King was with the Faqir, and that Faqir was a magician clairvoyant. Quoth he to the Parrot-King. "Go forth, your Majesty, to-day wilt thou regain thine own body." Meanwhile the hind had far outdistanced her pursuers.

Furthermore, my Master told me:

There lay a dead bear. The Vizir –King entered into the bear and pursued the hind, leaving the real King's body lying on the ground.

The news of the Vizir-King's coming was heard by the parrot. Thither did he run.

He waited, watching from a tree-hole.

He again entered into his own body;

wish ye him all good luck!

Hark ye, loyalty is monstrous rare.

Down fell the parrot dead., and the King entered his own body, but he who had been the Vizir was now in the bear. The real King mounted his horse, and said to his men. "Shoot ye that bear." They fired with their guns at him, and broke his leg. They seized him and brought him before the King. Said the King, "Treachery was done by thee to me. What can I do but kill thee? Otherwise people will say of me, 'He hath a bear for a Vizir.' Thou hast destroyed thine own body. Now no longer can I keep a bear like thee as a Vizir. Sir, I am about to kill thee."

And my Master further said,

They brought firewood, and they burnt the Vizir to ashes.

A hundred years passed, less or more.

And then came the messenger of Death to Bahadur Khan.

O Wahab*, the blacksmith, cry "Allah, Allah!"

Hark ye, loyalty is monstrous rare.

The belief in the possibility of external soul in animals is a recurring theme in all the folklore of Central Asia. The Shmans of Central Asia are belied to make use of this magical prowess in keeping their soul, or one of their souls, safe in the body of some animal. Frazer wrote about the notion of external soul prevalent in Central Asia:

'Nobody can find my external soul,' said one famous wizard, 'it lies hidden far away in the stony mountains of the Edzhigansk.' Only once a year, when the last snow melts and the earth turns black, do these external souls of wizards appear in the shape of animals among their dwellings. They wander everywhere, yet none but wizards can see them. The strong ones weep roaring and noisily, the weak steal about quietly and furtively. Often they fight, and then the wizard whose external soul is beaten falls ill or dies. The weakest and the most cowardly wizards are they whose souls are incarnate in the shape of dogs, for the dog gives his human double no peace, but gnaws his heart and tears his body. The most powerful wizards are they whose external souls have the shape of stallions, elks, black bears, eagles, or boars. Again, the Samoyeds of the Turukhinsk region hold that every shaman has a familiar spirit in the shape of a boar, which he leads about by a magic belt. On the death of the boar the shaman himself dies.[6]

In Kashmir, too, it is widely believed that an adept magician can transfix any human being or an animal in a pebble, a rock, a tree and the like. There are numerous tales in which the *jaadoogars* are shown with the power of petrifying a human being. Some stories even say that some of the big boulders are petrified people of the past and can come into life when the period of the punishment expires.

Most of the people in Kashmir and Central Asia have a tendency to worship fetishes of all kinds be a stone, an elm tree, a spring, a dilapidated tomb or anything associated with any saint of the past. They devise tales around the object of fetish and make the tales a part of their faith. Throughout Central Asia there are numerous shrines, places of worship, sacred springs, sacred boulders, sacred trees and other forms of fetishes and annual fetes are held in the name of the fetishes and totems. Ferry wrote about Afghanistan:

It is sufficient for an Afghan devotee to see a small heap of stones, a few rags, or some ruined tomb, something, in short, upon which a tale can be invented, to imagine at once that some saint is buried there. The idea conceived, he throws some more stones upon the heap and sticks up a pole or flag; those who come after follow the leader; more stones and more rags are added; at last its dimensions are so considerable that it becomes the vogue; a Mullah is always at hand with a legend which he makes or had revealed to him in a dream; all the village believes it; a few pilgrims come; crowds follow; miracles are wrought; and the game goes on, much to the satisfaction of the holy speculator, who drives a good trade by it, till some other Mullah more cunning than himself starts a saint of more recent date and greater miraculous powers, when the traffic changes hands. *

In Kashmir there is hardly a village without a fetish of this kind hallowed by some saint. The object of worship functions as a coveted symbol of identity of the village and serves as a force of unity among the villagers. In honour to the things of worship, people of the village distribute food of oblation *tahar* (boiled fried rice dyed by turmeric and mixed with fried leek and optionally, fried pieces of the flesh of the head of a goat or sheep) near it so that the spirit appropriating that thing is pleased. The cause of the event may be a nightmare or any kind of dream of any elder in the village. These things of reverence have played a historical role in the formation of tribes and communities and have also developed brotherhood and fellow-feeling among the members of the clan, village, or tribe. The fetishes are [7] components of cultural identity that ward off fears and conceived dangers.

Worship of the sainted dead has been prohibited by *shariat* (fundamental Islamic credos), but vouchsafed by Islamic mysticism. There are shrines and other places of worship associated with almost all the renowned Sufis and dervishes of Kashmir and Central Asia. Here is an anecdote from Idries Shah's *The Way of the Sufi*:

Saint-Worship

A Sufi sheikh was asked by a visitor:

'Is there any value in saint-worship?'

He at once said: 'It is illogical, and it is forbidden by Islam.' The inquirer went away, satisfied.

A disciple who had been present said: 'But your answer did not cover the implications of the question.'

The sheikh told him: 'The questioner was at the stage of Shariat (conventional religion). The way in which he put the question showed that that there was a certain reassurance which he wanted, and he sought it from me, of whom he had heard as a reliable source of opinion. There is however another kind of relationship with saints, one other than worship. Visiting their tombs has a virtue. But this virtue is operative only for those who can perceive it. This man was not one of them, so this other aspect of the question was void in his case.

'A man last month asked for verification of the fact that "cures wrought by shrine-meditation were entirely due to the aspiration, not the saint." I agreed with him. He had no capacity for more complex ideas: that in other words, this may be partly true on some occasions, wholly on others, and so on.

'It is characteristic of the blind that they can see only certain questions. Saints were men, visiting a shrine to some is bound to be "saint-worship", saint-worship is ignorant. Therefore there can be no advantage in saint-worship.

'One in a thousand, perhaps, who visits a shrine, will know inwardly why he is there and what is the nature of the virtue which he may derive from it. It is but natural that all pilgrims will imagine that they are "devout" and hence that they are all doing or experiencing exactly the same thing. Of course they are not. Have you ever tried to show a misguided man that his vision is narrow? He may listen to you in appearance. But for the sake of his own self-esteem he will reject what you mean, if not what you say.' (p. 231)

A universal theme of folk-literatures of the world is:

Kaavi Kuur (The Crow Girl)

One day two potters' wives went to the jungle to get a special kind of soil, which their husbands wanted for making some pots. They carried their infant children with them a-straddle on their hips. When they reached the place where this earth was to be found, they put down their children, a little boy and a little girl, to play together, while they filled their baskets. A kite and a crow noticed what was going on, and swooped down upon the children and carried them off. The kite killed the boy but the crow flew away with the girl to the hollow trunk of a tree in a distant part of the jungle, and there dropped her. Instead of crying the child thought it was great fun, and so laughed and played with the bird; and the bird got very fond of her, and brought her nuts and fruit, and scraps of bread and meat sometimes, whenever it could get them. The little girl grew up and became very beautiful.

One day a carpenter chanced to visit that part of the jungle for cutting wood. "Salam," said the girl to him, "I would like you to make me a spinning wheel. I am here all alone and I wish to do something."

"Why are you here? Where is your home? Have you no more clothes than the rag you are wearing?" asked the carpenter.

You must not ask me any questions," replied the girl. "But please make me a spinning wheel, and I shall be quite happy."

The carpenter did so; and the crow stole a spindle and some cotton for the girl. So she had everything complete.

Not long after this the king of that part of the world was out a-hunting in the jungle, and as he passed by that way, his hear caught the sound of somebody spinning. "Who resides in this solitary place?" he said to one of his attendants. "I hear the sound of spinning. Go and see who it can be." After a long search the men discovered the girl sitting by her wheel in the hollow of a tree, and brought her before the king. His majesty inquired everything about her; and was so interested in her story, and fascinated by her beauty, that he begged her to accompany him to the place, and to stay thee with him as his wife.

The king had six other wives. This crow girl was the seventh. Each of the wives had a separate apartment and special attendants. One day His Majesty, wishing to try their skill and taste, ordered all of them to decorate their rooms as well as they could. The six wives went to work in the ordinary way; they bought several ornaments and pictures, and had the walls of their rooms washed with attar of the roses; but the seventh wife sought an interview with her beloved crow and asked his advice on the matter. "Don't be anxious," said the bird, and immediately flew off and brought back in its bill an herb, which it gave her, saying, "Take this herb and rub it all over the walls of your room, and they will shine like burnished gold. "The girl obeyed, and her room shone so with gold___ real gold, that one could scarcely look at it.

When the king's other wives heard of this, they were very jealous. Notwithstanding they had washed their rooms with attar of roses, and decorated them with the richest carpets and the most magnificent vases, yet they looked not one hundredth part as beautiful as the crow girl's apartment. "What have you done to your room to make it so lovely?" they asked. But the crow girl did not tell them.

When the king inspected the rooms of the six wives, he was pleased with them, but when he came to the crow girl's room, he was overcome with astonishment and delight. Henceforth he made her his chief rani and seemed to forget all the rest.

The special notice from the king increased the hatred and jealousy of the other wives. They were wicked enough before; but now, maddened by the king's preference for the seventh wife, they plotted to bring about her speedy death. They soon found opportunity for accomplishing their wickedness. One day they were all going to the river to bathe, when it was decided to push the crow-girl queen into the water, and to inform the king that she had been accidentally drowned. Accordingly, when they reached a deep part of the river, they shoved the woman off the bank into water.

The king's grief was intense when he heard the sad news. For a long time he gave up all business, shut himself in his room, and would not see any one. Fate however, had not decreed the death of the rani. She was not drowned, as everybody thought. Near the part of the river where she fell, there happened to be a large tree growing out of an invisible island. He had floated to this island and climbed to the top of the tree, where she was constantly fed by her kind friend crow. One day some weeks afterwards His Majesty chanced to go for an airing in his boat by the way of this tree. The crow-girl saw him, and shouting the words, "the king unjustly exposed me to danger. Come, O beloved, come, here," she discovered herself to him. On seeing the beloved rani again, the king's joy knew no bounds. He immediately took her into the boat and carried her to the palace. There she told him all that had occurred, and when His Majesty heard the truth of the matter, he at once gave orders for the execution of other wives.[6]

Qissa Sangtaraash

In the legend of Sangtaraash a god-fearing sculptor of Kohi-Tuur makes a stony icon of God and keeps the icon on a citadel in a temple.

He worships the icon all the time and observes all rules of abstinence. One day while the devotee was away on some chore, prophet Moses passed by the temple. He demolished the temple and broke the icon. On this act of anger on the [11] devotee's naivety, God sent him His word of disapproval through Gabriel.

Mir Abdullah Baihaqi sermonises thus:

Haay luukoo saaryi khwati chhuv lool jaan
Looli siityiy zuv chhu laban musta'aan
Mir Abdullah chhu mangaan dwah ti raath
Lool eshqun tyiy dyitas ay paak zaat [12]

Tr. O people love is more precious than anything else

It is love that God gets His existence;
Mir Abdullah prays day and night,
"O God bestow true love on him!"

The transfer of Central Asian legends into Kashmiri continued in the nineteenth and the twentieth century and thus Kashmiri folk literature got enriched. Here is mention of some more popular legends of Central Asia in Kashmiri folk literature.

Zain Al-Arab

Zain al-Arab is the daughter of K'ab, the king of Qasdar, a city in ancient Afghanistan. She is exceptionally beautiful and a poet. K'ab receives several proposals for his daughter who is exceptionally beautiful. But her father wants o get her married to an equally good and heroic husband and thus rejects all proposals. Meanwhile K'ab dies, but before his death he advises his only son Harith to fulfil his wish.

On the occasion of his coronation, Harith receives guests from all the friendly countries. Harith has a servant, named Baktash, who is a beautiful and proficient musician. Baktash is ordered to sing for the delight of the guests. Hearing his song, Zain al-Arab falls in love with Baktash.

Zain al-Arab does not reveal her love for Baktash and pines inwardly. Harith seeks help from all the physicians, but nothing cures Zain al-Arab. Ultimately she divulges her secret to her most intimate maid. The maid takes her message to Baktash and he too begins to burn in the passion for her. Zain al-Arab composes beautiful love songs and sends them to Baktash who sings them.

One night Baktash somehow manages to enter the bed chamber of Zain al-Arab and implores for a night's pleasure. But Zain al-Arab tells him that her love is chaste and free from carnal desires. On Baktash's persistence, Zain al-Arab flees. The two lovers thus bear the pangs of separation, the essence of true love. Meanwhile the king of Qandhaar attacks Balakh. King Harith applies all his power to defend his country from the invader. Baktash, who like his other countrymen, fights the invading army, is seriously wounded. Zain al-Arab, disguised as a male soldier comes to the rescue of Baktash and saves him, without letting him know her identity. Amir-I Nasr, the king of Bukhara joins Harith against the invaders. Rudki, the great poet of Central Asia, was the poet laureate of the King of Bukhara.

The invaders are defeated and the there is great festivity in the country.

During the victory celebrations, Rudki meets Zain al-Arab. The two poets compete in versification and Rudki memorizes some of her verses. The guests depart.

Many days after this, Amir Nasr invites Harith Shah. Rudki, on the insistence of his master, sings some of the songs of Zain al-Arab. Amir Nasr is delighted to hear some new songs. Rudki tells his master that the songs are not his composition but that of Zain al-Arab. Amir Nasr gets impatient to see Zain al-Arab, but Rudki tells him that she is an immoral woman who loves a serf called Baktash. Harith Sha is infuriated to hear this, and in order to set things right, returns to his country. Baktash is arrested, and put into a dark abyss. Zain al-Arab is also imprisoned in a hot Hamam (a chamber kept by steam). She suffers all the pain of simmering heat and confinement and writes her pathetic songs of separation on the walls of the Hamaam. She eventually dies. After her burial, Baktash is released from the dark hole. When the news of Zain al-Arab's death is broken to him, he in a fit of wrath stabs Harith Shah to death. He sings mournful songs at the grave of his beloved and slays himself at the spot.

The tragic legend of Zain al-Arab, is a part of Kashmiri folklore was been rendered into the form of a *mathnavi* by Abdul Ahad Nazim (Bijbihara, Kashmir: 1816-1851).

Gulrez

In the famous city of Nakhshab of Persia, there lived a prince, called Maasum Shah, who was the only son of the king, named Faghfuur. One day while taking delight of a musical concert, Maasuum Shah saw a strange bird in the tree near his window. The bird was so attractive that the prince longed to catch it and put it in a golden cage. His courtiers tried to dissuade him, but he was so furious that he stood up and began shaking his body. As a result of this a few pearls got detached from his crown and fell on the carpet. The queer bird in the tree anon came down to peck at the pearls. The courtiers thus knew what the bird ate. They set a snare and spread pearls over it. The bird was caught in the snare. The prince was so engrossed in the strange habits of the bird that he continued gazing at it.

After a few days the bird in the cage stopped eating any food and looked morose. Seeing this, the prince grew anxious and wanted to know the reason. When the bird saw the prince in distress, it narrated its tale of woe. The bird told the prince that it could make him happy had it been in its original form. But also it had undergone metempsychosis under a curse.

The bird tells the prince that she is essentially a princess, called Noshlab and belonged to a country called Baitul Aman. Her father's name is Mashhoor Shah and her mother's name is Gulbadan. The bird further tells the prince that a prince of Turkistan, named Ajab Malik was in love with her as he had heard praises of her beauty through a traveller. Ajab Malik had abdicated the palace and set out on a sea journey in search of her. He was accompanied by many friends, but his ship was wrecked in the ocean. All had perished in the sea, except Ajab Malik who sailed on a piece of the broken ship and reached an island where he discovered a Pari imprisoned in a grotto. He had set her free by killing the monster who had abducted her. The name of the Pari was Nazmast, who was none other than a close friend of Noshlab.

Thus Noshlab, in the shape of the encaged bird, continues to narrate that her friend Nazmast came to know the identity of Ajab Malik and his problem. She managed to arrange for a meeting between Noshlab and Ajab Malik in a garden. The lover and beloved, thus united consummated their desire and promised to lead a married life. Noshlab further tells the prince that while she was busy making love with her lover in the garden and satisfying her carnal desire, her mother saw her in that awkward condition. While the lover and the beloved were in deep slumber, her mother in rage got Ajab Malik, the love-lorn prince, arrested and exiled to Turkistan while he was asleep. Noshlab too in her slumber was taken away and kept confined in her bed chamber in the palace. Noslab, when awake, yelled and wept, but her mother did not take pity on her. She on the contrary cast a spell on her and changed her into a bird to wander about. She had been in the form of a bird for twenty long years and flew from country to country in search of her love, Ajab Malik.

Maasuum Shah thus knew the secret of the queer bird and took the encaged bird to Baitul Aman. He persuaded the parents of Ajab Mailk to arrange the marriage of Ajab Malik and Noshlab.

After a series of interesting episodes and twists in the story, Nosh Lab gets transformed into her original human form and her marriage is finalized with Ajab Malik. Eventually Maasuum Shah, too, gets married to the bosom friend of Noshlab. Ajab Malik's friend Rasikh also finds a bride, Mastnaz, the younger sister of Nazmast. All the reunited lovers happily return to their respective countries.

The legend of Gulrez is the most popular tale in Kashmiri because of its beautiful poetic rendering by a late nineteenth century poet Maqbool Shah (Kraalawor, Kashmir: (?-d. 1877). It may be pointed out here that the original Persian tale is in prose, recorded by Zia Nakhshabi.*

Zuhra And Behram

The romance concerns the love story of Bahram, the only son of the King of Baglana. His love affair starts from his school in which the daughter of the Vazir of the country; her name is Zuhra. The Vazir did not like Bahram's advances towards his daughter at that tender age and thus stopped her from attending that school. He also complained to the king that his son had seduced his innocent daughter. The king in his rage ordered the prince's exile.

Bahram used his old maid servant in sending a secret message to Zuhra. She helps Zuhra leave her father's house secretly in the morning and run off with Behram towards a desert.

The Vazir orders his men to follow the fleeing lovers and get the Prince arrested. The tired eloped lovers reach an oasis and they come down from the horse to have rest. Zuhra eventually falls asleep and Behram remains guarding her. A lion attacks them, but the prince valiantly fights, the lion, chases it and finally kills it at a distance. Zura wakes up, finding no trace of the prince there, she rides towards the desert in search of him. Meanwhile, Behram returns to the spot, and finding no trace of Zura there, is much perturbed. The two lovers thus set out in two directions in search of each other.

After several days' solitary journey, Zuhra reaches a beautiful garden of a country and wants to have a sojourn there. The prince of that country chances to see her in the garden and falls in live with her at first sight. But Zuhra does not reciprocate and tells the prince of the country she is a wayfarer, detached from her caravan and that her name is Khirdmand. The prince invites her to his palace and arranges a feast in her honour.

At night the prince and his friends get drunk and assault Zuhra. The latter bravely defends her chastity and flees carrying the prince's crown on her head.

Zuhra, disguised as a man, reached another country and took refuge in the house of a woman. She tells her host that "he" was a merchant, "his" caravan was looted by pirates and "he" managed to save "his" life. Zurha disguised as a young man stayed in the country. The fame of her beauty spread all around and the princess of the country fell in love with her, disguised as a young man. Zuhra, too, continued to retain her disguise.

One day she, disguised as a young man, on the pretext of of hunting she leaves the country so that she could make search for her lost lover, Behram. A king of yet another country sees her (him). He likes him / her and, having no son of his own, offers her/him to be his son. Zuhra reflects and for certain gains accepts the king's offer. The king wants to get his only daughter married to her/him. Zuhra somehow convinces the king to postpone the marriage for one year. Meanwhile the king dies and she (as the adopted son) ascends the throne.

One day, while on an errand of hunting, Zuhra now disguised as the new king) chances to find a Youngman, but worn out and emaciated. She recognizes him as her own lover Behram. Zuhra orders her men to carry Behram to the palace where she arranges for energizing food and regal robes for him. She then reveals her true self to Behram. She gets married to her lover. The actual princess of the country goes mad to see this, but Zuhra being magnanimous, allow Behram to have her as second wife. Behram thus becomes the prince of a new country.

The story of Zura and Behram is full of funny and dramatic twists. The whole interest lies in the mistaken identity of Zuhra, as male and as female. Mistaken identity of people is yet another recurring theme of Central Asian legends and folk tales.

The story of Zuhra and Behram has been rendered into a poem by Aashaq Trali (Tral: ?-d. 1910).

Shirin Wa Khusrav

The haunting story of *Shirin wa Khusrav* has been a popular legend in Kashmir since Mehmood Gami (Memoodabad: 1755-1850) adapted it from Abu'r Rahman Jami's *mathnavi* of the same title.

Khusrav Parvez is the only son of Hurmuz, the son of Navshirvan of Iran. He has been born to his parents after many religious rituals, prayers and offerings at various shrines. Khusrav Parvez grows up as a young man of unparalleled beauty. In his early teens he happens to hear about the virtues and beauty of Shireen, the daughter of a rich lady of Arman. The praises of Shireen silently move Khurav Parvez to uncontrollable love for the paragon of beauty, Shireen. He eventually sends Shahvoor, his friend to Arman to motivate Shireen to visit his palace.

Shahvoor stealthily enters Shireen's garden and keeps a portrait of Khusrav hanging on a tree there. When Shireen sees the portrait she grows crazy over the bewitching beauty of Khusrav Parvez. She asks Shahvoor for the address of Khusrav Parvez and Shavoor gives her a ring of Khusrav Parvez so that she could find him easily.

Riding her horse, named Shabdez, Sheerin travels to Khusrav Parvez's country. Meanwhile, Khusrav Parvez's minister Behram maligns him before his father who is enraged. Khusrav Parvez runs away from his palace and takes refuge in Shireen's house in Arman. When Shireen reaches Khusrav Parvez' palace, she shows his parents the ring that was sent to her. She is well treated there. Meanwhile Khusrav Parvez's father dies and he returns to his country and ascends the throne. During this time, Shireen returns to her home, where she does not find Khusrav Parvez.

Behram, the minister of Khusrav Parvez becomes a rebel and makes Khusrav Parvez flee his country. He again takes refuge in Shireens house at Arman. Shireen motivates Khusrav Parvez to take revenge on Behram and recover his power. Khusrav Parvez follows her advice and attacks Behram and defeats him. He assumes the rule of his country. In the meantime, Shireen's mother also dies and Shireen assumes power. Khusrav Parvez sends his friend Shavor to get Shireen for him.

A parallel story emerges when a stone-cutter, named *Farhaad* or *Kohkan* (= stone-cutter) emerges as another ardent lover of Shireen. Shireen's only diet is milk of goats, but it would take a very long time to fetch milk from the pastures that are located behind a hill, called Beestone. Khusrav Parvez, therefore, orders Farhaad the stone-cutter to dig a channel across the hill so that milk flows through it to Shireen's palace. Since Farhad the stone-cutter, though convinced of the stupendous ordeal, accepts the challenge to give expression to the ardour of his love for Shireen; he digs the channel. But he demands

Shireen as a reward for the accomplishment. Khusrav Parvez in his perplexity spreads a rumour that Shireen has died suddenly. On hearing this rumour, Farhad in a fit of shock kills himself with his own hammer. Shireen is much bereaved on the sad end of her ardent lover. However, she lives with Khusrav Parvez.

Khusrav Parvez has a son by his earlier wife. He imprisons him and then kills him. Shireen in her disress commits suicide.

The tragic story of Khusrav Parvez and Shireen, also known as the story of *Shiree wa Farhaad* has become an integral part of Kashmiri folk literature. There are numerous songs in which the allusion of Shiree and Farhaad occur that signify the purity of passionate love.[15]

The tale has been rendered into *mathnavis* by Mehmood Gami. After him, the tale was also rendered into a drama by Ghulam Nabi Dilsoz in the fifth decade of the twentieth century.

Like the *Dastan*s discussed above, there are many other Dastans in Kashmiri which have descended down to us through the oral medium. Although there are traces of this dying art is still traceable in the countryside, but it is being fast replaced by modern electronic media, like Radio and Television. However, it is the inherent strength of this art that it is adaptable by other form of entertainment. A successful experiment was made by Ghulam Nabi Dilsose in the fifties of the last century when he rendered some most popular Dastans into dramas and taking advantage of the then new medium of folk appeal that is a gramophone, got them recorded in the voices of characters. His dramatic versions were first published by a local publisher, and now in his Kulyati Dilsose.

As we saw all these Dastans are full of many dramatic situations when the the characters are involved in action and the emotions are fully charged. This features of these Dastans have been exploited by some of our playwrights, like Dinanath Nadim, Amin Kamil, Moti Lal Keemu, Makhan Lal Saraf and others and produced dramatic versions of the legends. In the next chapter we shall discuss some of these experiments in detail.

Part I. Dastangoi as a Complement to Vocal Delivery

In the last chapter we saw how numerous *Dastan*s in the Kashmiri language are rich in dramatic element that has been used by various repertories of the traditional folk theatre to entertain as well as inform the audience. In the present chapter we shall try to see the scope of using *Dastan* as a technique of making the vocal delivery of modern theatre an effective element. Vocal delivery is one of the principal elements of all drama that has to be commensurate with the performance. It is interesting to quote from one of the most admirable plays of Shakespeare that is *Hamlet*:

> "… suit the action to the word and the word to the action, with this special observance that you o'erstep not the modesty of nature." (*Hamlet* III.ii)

We must bear in mind that the *Dastan* is essentially a product of the oral culture, whereas modern theatre is radically visual. In modern drama Performance text tends to replace dramatic text. Yet the art of story-telling when accompanied by performance makes the scene very effective in having the desired effect on the audience. The actors in a modern drama rarely follow the instructions of the writer, they continuously experiment with enlivening their action by various techniques that include conventional narratives wherever necessary. Many theoreticians of modern drama like Stanislavski, Brecht, Grotowski and many others have experimented in making modern drama an art form rife with many ingredients of traditional arts including story-telling to make acting and vocal delivery interdependent.

Old society relied on oral expression and as such rhetoric played a central role in theatrical performances. Effective vocal delivery imbibed strength from narration which was highly accentuated by various methods of voice modulations.

Since all *Dastans* belong to a shared fund of the society, modern theatre has experimented in exploiting this shared memory to intensify action and so that the stark representation of various social problems like violence, exploitation, intimidation, fear, and ennui is made palatable as a theatrical reality. The audience is made more and more conscious that theatrical performance is not reality but a verisimilitude of reality based on art. Narration in the style of tradition *Dastan* has proved an effective tool in making modern drama an artistic representation of reality.

Drama, like life, is in fact a composite art in which the written word of the playwright is concretised when it becomes the spoken word of the actor on the stage, but it is closely associated with the many other aspects of life and can efficiently combine all other arts in concretizing an abstract idea. *Daastan* too, prior to drama remained for several millennia a composite art in which the narrator is assisted by performing artists, dancers, and singers. Thus *Dastan* being timeless in import can be easily merged in drama to attain the desired end, educative, entertainment, politics, cultural awareness of national assertion. It has been increasingly turning to history, legend, myth and folklore, tapping their springs of vitality and vocal cords of popularity with splendid results. Like other advanced countries in India too many innovative theatre personalities have exploited the efficacy of folktales and romances of love, adventure, and magic in energising their plays. Girish Karnad, Mohan Rakesh, Badal Sircar and Vijay Tendulakar are the most eminent theatre personalities who have paved the way for using various communicative modes as forms of vocal delivery in contemporary drama.

The traditional form of vocal delivery is the dialogue, and all the dialogues are situational, depending on the mood of the speaker, nature of the audience, and the overall context. In view of this shortcoming of the vocal delivery, many major changes in the ideal vocal delivery have been introduced by various dramatists and directors of stage drama. Their various notions have resulted in a multiplicity of approaches of acting and dialogues spoken by the actors. The general trend in modern theatre is to liberate the action from the traditional rhetoric of dialogues so that the mood, nature, age, emotional state and other individual traits of actors do not tell upon the general purport of a scene in a drama and the total effect. Attempt has been made to create such a theatre as is free from the limitations of the actors and the audience and is autonomous and polyphonic.

One of the innovators in this direction was Stanislavski who presented his theory of subtext. He emphasised emotional memory and physical actions. He evolved his own system, which was well structured. He said that words of dialogues did not contain the full meaning, but all the words depended on what lay beneath them. The deep-level meaning, different from surface meaning was the real essence and needed to be made fully operational. In his opinion the sub-text was more important that the given text. Often the surface text being too shallow does not create any impact as the audience is not attentive to it. Thus text was considered part of the creative process, and an integral part of action, and no longer a literary form.

One of the methods of Stanislavski was to master voice and text in order to convey all the connotative and denotative aspects of speech while the actor was involved in a situation of the stage. This necessitated rigorous training to have full control on pitch, diction, articulation and accent so that all the aspects of oral communication are made servile to the pre-planned motifs of the scene as well as action. In spite of the rigorous training and directors instruction all the ingredients of the vocal delivery were subjective and hardly matched the original experience to be presented physical before audience of variegated nature in terms of age, maturity, status, social prejudices, affiliations, political allegiance and emotional composition. Director regularizes and determines intonation, pauses, emphasis on key words, ellipsis, and use of silence in the vocal delivery, yet he has to depend on the competence of the actors; he/she cannot create an entirely new actor of his own notions. Stanislavski wrote:

> The habit of speaking in measures will make your speech more graceful in form, intelligible and profound in content, because it forces you to keep your mind constantly on the essential meaning of what you are saying when you are on the stage. Until you achieve this, there is no use either in your attempting to carry out one of the principal functions of the words, which is to convey the illustrated subtext of your monologue, or even in doing the preparatory work of creating this subtext.

This method too has its limitations because the linguistic competence varies from person to person. The application of the rules of the language depends on the speaker's conscious knowledge of moulding the rules of grammar and lexis to give perspective. Stanislavski wrote:

With us we have as many planes of speech which create perspective in a phrase. The most important word stands out most vividly defined in the very foreground of the sound plane. Less important words create a series of deeper planes.

Brecht held a very different notion of vocal deliver; it was closely related to his theory of non-illusionistic theatre, what he called epic theatre. It was against Stanislavski's theory of vocal delivery and theory of sub-texts. In order to liberate theatre from the preferences, competences and psychological traits of the actors, Brecht suggested that the theatre should include various techniques of descriptions, references, commenting choruses and even written projections. All that was needed was to make a dramatic situation "artistically demonstrated". His concept of "artistic demonstration" was to highlight and intensify the desired effect through various comments and judgements. He fundamentally wanted that drama should play a role in social transformation towards higher consciousness of the problems of this mundane world. For this purpose a theatrical performance could merge various auxiliary techniques such as the narratives, anecdotes from history, small interludes, parables, fables, proverbs and other items of the repertoire of inherited memory passed on from generation to generation through oral media. Brecht thus took a bold departure from the Aristotelian form which was based on classical unities, unity of action and a well-structured plot. Since modern drama has to be about the common man of the rural or urban life beset with various agricultural or industrial injustices, drama has to accept all the forms of linguistic and para-linguistic activities that assist the process of bringing home the analysis of the worldly problems.

Brecht believed that the stage should become a site of busy activities. While agreeing with Aristotle that the story must remain the nucleus of the drama, he advocated narrative realism. His notion of narrative realism was neither naturalism, nor symbolism, but something between the two or a combination of the two. The audience should feel that they are not watching a slice of reality, nor an arbitrary substitute of a piece of reality but a piece of the theatrical reality. While being based on social issues, a drama has to be a drama, something that is manipulated through the director, and the actors and other performers. Thus Brecht liberated the dramatic performance from the dull faithfulness to the textual words, phrases and sentences. The audience should feel constantly conscious of the distance between actual life and a dramatic representation which has to be achieved through vibrant collaboration of many other arts, like story-telling, comments through proverbs, anecdotes, humour, side-talks, reference to history, romance, and other collective memory matrix. Brecht did not consider the verbal text of a play to be sacrosanct, but something that opened up the possibilities of the contribution of theatrical persons. In theorising this kind of epic drama, Brecht never accepted anarchy on the stage but an organic inter-relationship of various elements of communication.

One of the kernel concepts of Brecht's theory of epic theatre is his idea of the "alienation effect". This concept means that that the dramatis personae should use sufficient empathy in performance, but at the same time convince the audience that they are involved in representation of the behaviour of men and women, the purpose must be to win the audience's sympathies. Similarly the performers on the stage should remain always alert that they are being watched by an audience of diverse nature. While performing, the performer has to be intensely conscious that there is a distance between his actual personality and the personality he or she is representing on the stage. He should therefore look at himself or herself from a distance.

Brecht supported definite techniques which he called 'gestus'. By gestus he meant that all the elements of the verbal structure of a specific written play should not remain a dead matter like classical drama, by a living stuff which could be re-energised through vivacious gestus which depended on the choice of the performer. He emphasised 'gestic' rhythms not stiff textual rhythms of the written text. It is the gestic rhythm that varies from performance to performance of the same play. Thus, according to Brecht, one could have a new Shakespeare play in every new performance of the same play. This is the secret of his greatness. It is said that 'every age has a new Shakespeare'; we can say that every performance discovers or invents a new Shakespeare. Not only the nature of the audience but also the performers play an integral role in determining the import of a play, the social reality changes and the import also changes.

The technique of Dastan could easily be used as a comment on the action, the situation and moral or political motives. This not only breaks the usual monochromatic dialogue delivery, but also aids communication. As Brecht believed that the 'gestus' could predominate by allowing the actors to speak in the third person and in the past. His characters used to speak all the stage directions and comments while acting. He allowed his actors to adopt a well-developed speech which was well trained to express hidden passions. The actors were also encouraged to use their various social and cultural dialects and not the frigid literary language. Thus the Dastan has immense scope in achieving this purpose.

The epic nature of Brecht's plays encompasses all the sections, classes, and dialects, as well as the cultural items like the bard's singing, the introduction of sub-plot that enhance the effect of a situation in the form of allegories. There is also the possibility of introducing traditional musical accoutrements like traditional musical instruments, costumes, mime show and masquerade. In this way every theatrical performance becomes a multi-layered and multi-directional activity that, like a true epic, involves as well as represents the whole society of a particular historical period, and thus assumes a national character. Variety and variegated nature of acting, performing, playing and soliloquising and chorus help a theatrical event achieve the desired effect towards a desired social consciousness, individual reflection and decision-making. All this is achieved delightfully without the austerity of rhetoric and propaganda.

The traditional *Dastan* when assimilated skilfully in the corpus of a theatrical performance, the audience is assisted in analysis of problems and arriving at conclusions of their own. It does not become a unidirectional and passive act of watching which a spectacle of any other form of physical performance like acrobatics aims at. Reflection, introspection, analysis and inferences are the ultimate purpose of creative art. In modern drama all this achieved without remaining servile to the traditional procedures of vocal delivery that were readymade and neatly designed to be delivered by the actor. The actors need not be passive agents, but participating human forces to decide the nature of the characters and their interactions. The human aspect of a theatrical performance is enhanced manifold by the combination of various communicative arts, particularly the story-telling or *Dastan* in our context.

The art of the *Dastan* could certainly help the actors to maintain a duality in his acting. Brecht desired that the actors should on the one hand relive the life of the characters assigned to each of them, and, on the other hand, live and represent his/her own personality on the stage. This is what Stanislavski called "perspective of the role and the perspective of the actor." Brecht's notion of this duality was different from Stanislavski in the sense that he (Brecht) deliberately introduced the techniques which helped actors in passing from prose to verse and from speech to song. The maximum use this technique was in the staging of Brecht's *Mother Courage*, in which he introduced his personal instructions to make it altogether different from the Shakespearean model in which vocal delivery deliberately aims at catharsis of actors. He wished that his audience should get a 'chronicle' form of *Mother Courage* for it was based on factual details in specific frameworks of time and space. He tried to obstruct emotional identification with the characters so that drama looks like a complex combination of various conscious techniques, not a slice of life. The kernel importance of the drama on stage has to be in the art of combination, not in realistic representation. Thus there is scope of introducing elements of all forms of art, particularly song, dance, narration and masquerade. The *Dastan goi* as an independent art form, too, could be assimilated and introduced at relevant places so that drama on the stage attains maximum effect in vocal delivery.

Element of traditional narratives, like *Dastan* plays another significant role. It can easily bridge the gaps of time and space. There are many dramas in which there is switching over of scenes from the factual level to the fictional level. Shakespeare's King Lear is the best example of this which violates the unities of place and unities of time. Many scenes in the play are mere poetry for being based on poetic imagination rather than interplay of character and incident. Shakespeare knew this and as such complemented his dramas with a variety of auxiliary vocal deliveries like the songs, chorus, fool, soliloquy and reporting. Brecht's epic theatre resolves this physical limitation through interplay of heterogeneous elements belonging to various arts so that the audience achieves suspension of disbelief which in Coleridge's concept he considered the most vital part of all imaginative works. When, for instance, the protagonist in a drama is confined to such a position as belongs to the past or to some imaginary landscape, the narrator comes to the foreground to bridge the gap between the two times and two lands. The narrator of *Dastangoi* can use his craft to assist suspension of disbelief in the audience who live in a real time, that is in a hall observing the events of the past on a physical stage. If there is a drama in which the lover and beloved are separated from each other by some supernatural power and there is no dramatic method to work out their reunion, a segment of *Dastangoi* can easily be incorporated in the stage performance of that situation. Here is for instance the very beginning of the most celebrated *mathnavi* in Kashmiri, titled *Gulrez*. A lovelorn prince, named M'asoom Shah is enticed by a strange but highly charming bird. He like a true pampered prince is obstinate to have the bird in his cage. He is informed by his wise Wazir that the bird in the tree eats nothing but precious pearls. On hearing this the prince unropes a handful of pearls of his necklace and offers it as a bait to the bird. The bird readily comes through the window to peck at the pearls and is thus caught and caged. The bird now in the cage and kept for the joy of the prince, starts narrating its tale. The bird reveals to him that it is originally a princess who is jinxed by her cruel mother for having slept with her lover, a prince, named Ajab Malik who is sent to some deserted island. The lovelorn prince M'asoom Shah, moved by the sad tale, assures the bird that he would face all ordeals to find out the princess's lover (the bird in the cage) and seek the reunion of the separated lovers. … The beginning, although quite dramatic, is a situation that is impossible to stage and covers many past events. This interesting situation can be easily made credible through the narration of *Dastangoi* when the drama is to be presented on the stage….

This technique of interpolating in stage or television drama can easily be followed in other tales of fantasy and imagination. In the next section we shall discuss and analyse how *Dastangoi* is actually used as a technique in some modern dramas in Kashmiri.

Before we discuss how *Dastangoi* is used in contemporary Kashmiri drama, or see its scope of as an effective strategy, it is important to keep in mind that every *Dastan* or folk tale has had its origin in a particular milieu of a social group and an attempt to reproduce it in a different milieu and time means that it cannot be expected to have the same impact on the audience. Many things get lost in every effort of reproduction: the mythic element, approach to natural and supernatural powers, interaction between the human and the non-human forces, the ethical values, the aesthetic values, the aspects of material culture such as dress, diet, household items, the language, kinship, family structure, and even the fauna and flora. An example of this loss of substance in transferring the tale of an alien land of a remote time to a modern audience through drama is the story of Laila and Majnoon, an ancient folk tale of the Arab world which has gained tremendous popularity in the Ajam (non-Arab world) too. The story, though entirely strange to Kashmiri people, has remained a household tale, and has been reproduced in the form of drama too. The story is so well known that it sounds redundant to summarise here, nevertheless, the story goes:

> Majnoon, also named Qais, was a lovelorn young man of ancient Arabia, who was enchanted by the black beauty of Laila, meaning 'dark night". Being gifted by nature, he expressed his passions for Laila in the form of songs that became popular among the masses. It was the ardour of his romantic passion that got him the nickname 'Majnoon', meaning a frenzied person. He approached Laila's father to seek her hand, but he was rebuked for being considered a madman. Laila, on reaching her adulthood was married into a rich family to a handsome and robust person, named Al-Thaqafi, nicknamed 'ward' which in Arabic means a red rose.

On hearing about this marriage, Majnoon could no more contain his ardent love, renounced his home and began wandering in a wilderness, called Najd. All the efforts of his parents failed in persuading him to return and he continued singing about his desire for Laila, About the fate of Laila, there are many versions of the story, but the most accepted version says that she died of heart break for seeing her lover die of getting stoned by the mindless folks. Majnoon clung close to the grave of Laila and died there. It is said that the people then got moved by his tragic end and buried him beside the grave of Laila, the only goal of his life. The story of the undying love of Majnoon is rife with many mystic meanings, and poets of all time in the East have written the tale in many long and moving narratives. In Kashmiri, too, there are several versified narratives about the incident, but the most popular version of the *Dastan* is that of Mahmood Gami, who wrote it in the second half of the nineteenth century in the form of numerous lyrics roped together by narrative passages.

The traditional artists in *daastangoi* have sung this romance of Mahmood Gami in their own way. "The story is no less than an opera," wrote Naji Munawar, the compiler of Mahmood Gami's collected works. Mahmood Gami was conversant with the story through two versions of the Dastan, one by Rudaki, and the other by Nizami Ganjawi. It is said that there are as many as 1000 versions of the Dastan of Laila and Majnnon in Persian that are still extant in the libraries of Iran.

Thus we see that repeated reproduction of the story by various individuals, poets or traditional artists in *daastangoi* have taken every kind of license in narrating the incidents, names, visual imagery, under-currents of mystic love, the surroundings, the locale and all other references to the time and space. This phenomenon of changes in the rendering of *daastangoi* are universally accepted principles of narrative art.

The story of Laila and Majnoon was, quite rich in dramatic events, was reproduced as theatrical performances by some dramatic repertories in the first half the twentieth century. However, the very first play-version of the narrative was written by Ghulam Nabi Dilsoze who used the audio version of the dialogues and popularised it through his gramophone.

The undying narrative of Laila and Majnoon in the form of a theatrical performance opens with the wild songs of a young and robust youth against the backdrop of a street thronged by people, all gazing at him and leaving with a sarcastic smile on their faces.

Majnoon, indifferent to people's jibes continues singing while looking towards the half-shut window of Laila, the song goes like this:

Sih eesith sapnus shaaloo, ami pyalay banyov mya kyah
Soor rovum mwal kyiho maaloo, ashqi tsuuran kornam dah,
Ashqi doaduy bo kithis tsaalo, ami pyalay banyov mya kyah
Sar bi vandihay yitmo saal, haal vuchtam banyov mya kyah,
Shahbaazah log kyah zaalo, ami pyalay banyov mya kyah.
Chaanyi keetiri paan bo gaalo, manz maedani rovum rah,
Yiti karihay poshan maaloo, ami pyalay banyov mya kyah.
Ashqi kyitaabyi vuchto faalo, gatyi andray haavtam mah,
Katyi tshandath paniney laalo, ami pyalay banyov mya kyah.

Trans.

{A lion I was now am turned into a jackal, oh what an effect this goblet has had on me! I quaffed the wine cup after cup. I lost all, what principal I should care about, the burglar of love has ransacked me; How shall I endure this ailment of love? I shall lay down my head at your feet, but, once, for once, care to see my condition. See how the eagle is languishing in the snare. Come I shall adorn you with many a garland. Just look for the omen in the book of love, and show me your radiant face in the dark. O my love where shall I wander in search of you? What an effect the goblet has had on me!}

Enamoured by Majnoon's songs, Laila, entreats him secretly in her chamber with the pretext that he was a 'mot' or a wonder-working dervish. The lover and the beloved spend some time, but the more she satiated him, the more mad he grew for her.

The family members and the neighbours and other folks of the tribe somehow come to know about this secret union of the two and they grow mad with wrath. The mad lover is punished and forced to go into the wilderness.

Though it is not quite easy to depict this scene of union on the stage, yet modern electronic media are quite viable for this kind of situation. Proper sound effects, music in the background and the sobs of the two lovers could re-create the passionate scene. In the folk media on the stage this impediment is overcome with the narrative singing of the *Dastangoi.* He used to function as a chorus, as we have, in the Western drama, and the narrative rendering makes such scenes all the more fascinating because they kindle the imagination of the audience to envision the scene individually according to individual imagination. Physical representation generally mars the effect of such scenes as the audience is subservient to the imagination of the stage director.

There are a few potent dramatic scenes in the narrative of Laila and Majnoon. Some of the most dramatic scenes are:

Laila's wedding with the rose-faced young man of some tribe. And the ensuing revelry in the tribe.
Majnoon, sent to the wilderness, wanders aimlessly, craving for a drop of water.
Mindless folks stoning him and tearing his clothes.
Laila is informed about the miseries of Majnoon.
Laila disappears in the family and the resulting commotion.
Laila is seen applying balm on the wounds of Majnoon in the wilderness.
Majnoon is in his death throes and Laila's grief.
Laila dies near the sandy-grave of Majnoon.

Thus we see that the narrative of a distant land of Arabia, assumes the local colour in terms of all the details. Being an archetypal tale of devastating passion, annihilation, and metaphoric re-union, Laila and Majnoon shall remain a permanent theme of the theatre as well as the electronic media in future also.

The Daastann of Yousuf and Zulaikha, though a part of the sacred book of the Quran, has been rendered into a *Dastan* for the first time by the celebrated Persian poet Jami. (1414-1492), a Sufi poet.

His version of Yousuf Zulaikha, is certainly based on some pre-existing version of the story from the oral medium. He takes many licenses in making the story moving and has introduced his poetic imagination and art of rhetoric in making the Dastan an immortal piece of literature. In Kashmir, profoundly influenced by Persian narrative poetry, especially of Jami and Nizami, too has made the story the subject of his immortal *mathnavi*, titled 'Yousud Zulaikha. It was the tremendous popularity of Mahmood Gami's *mathnavi*, that numerous copies of his manuscript were prepared and circulated even in his own lifetime. It was the literary merit of the *Dastan* that famous German orientalist Karl Burkhard translated Mahmood's poem into German in 1875. Since then the *Dastan* has been heard and enjoyed apart from its scriptural connotations and has remained a recurring theme of many traditional storytellers and poets. Each version deviates from the original not only in diction, but also in the series of events and metaphors. Here is the summary of the tale that is almost common to all versions. Since the *Dastan* has a Quranic background, no attempt has been made to dramatise it, but the Dastan singers continue narrating it through the oral medium. Each individual rendering is different from the previous one, although the basic plot remains unaltered. They deviate and show variety in terms of style, expression of emotions, and imagery. The Quranic version of the Dastan is unchangeable. The story given in summary form in Surah xii is not mentioned by the poets and the singers of the narratives. The story appears in only 11 *Aayats*, i.e., 23-32, and 51 of the Surah. The protagonist Zulaikhah in Jami's poem and in other adaptations, like Mahmood Gami's, she assumes more significance in terms of poetic demands, like figurative expression, human passion, conflicts, and her roles in society and family. In this sense Yousuf looks like a flat, or two dimensional character, who is loved and being treated variously by various characters, like his brother, his seller, Zulaikha, and his father. He has no conflict and the result of mere narration. Jami and other poets have added the non-scriptural events out of the folk memory.

Among the secular tales, that is the tales not found in the Quran, have been drastically altered and alterations are the principle of their continuity. Nizami's long poem *Sheereen wa Khusrav* was for the first time adapted in Kashmiri by Mahmood Gami in the second half of the eighteenth century. He has certainly abbreviated it in his adaptation and reduced many details in the original; his rendering can be taken as original as it is not a faithful translation but a creative adaptation of trans-creation. In the original poem we see that the story begins with Khusrav's birth and schooling. The next episode in the *Dastan* is his feast in a farmer's house which annoys his father, named Hormizd.

While Khusrav in his adolescence was in his grandfather's house, he dreams that he is given the hand of an exceptionally pretty bride, named Shirin, a horse named Shabdiz, and a musician, named Barbad. And a vast kingdom called Persia. Khusrav has a friend named Shapur who is a gifted painter. He tells him that Shirin is the niece of an Armenian queen, Mahin Banu. His friend uses all his mastery of depicting the details of a human form, and describes the visage of Shirin. It is the description of the princess that enamours Khusrav and falls in love with Shirin without seeing her in her real form. Performing the duty of a true friend Shapur travels to Armenia and shows his painting of Khusrav to Shirin, and she eventually falls in love with him. She secretly flees her land and reaches Khusravs land, named Mada'in. In the meantime, Khusrav too flees his father's land and reaches Armenia in search of Shirin. The two lovers even happen to meet on their way to their separate destinations, but being in disguise do not recognise each other.

On reaching Armenia, Khurav receives a warm welcome from Shamira, the queen of the land. He comes to know that Shirin has fled to Madain, and Shapur is sent to get her back. When Shirin returns to her native land, Khusrav is away to his own native land as his ailing father has died in his grief. Thus the two lovers are seen travelling in opposite directions. It happens that Khusrav is dethroned by a warlord, and he flees to Armenia. He is welcomed by Shirin, but does not agree to marry him and asks him to re-conquer his lost kingdom. Being ardent in his love, he promises Shirin that he would return to Armenia after defeating his enemy. He seeks help from Caesar, but the latter agrees to help him on the condition that he marries his daughter, Maryam. He agrees and makes a promise to Caesad that he would never re-marry so long as Mariam lives. Maryam knows all about his love for Shirin and makes sure that he never sees her again.

A reputed sculptor, named Farhad, falls in love with Shirin. When Khusrav comes to know about Farhad's love, he out of jealousy send him into exile to the Behiston mountain and assigns him an impossible ordeal of digging out a river of milk through the cliffs. Undaunted in his love, Farhad accepts the challenge and is engaged in the impossible task.

In the meantime, Khusrav sends false news to Farhad that Shirin has died. On hearing this news, Farhad, who has already made considerable progress, is hocked by the news and jumps down a cliff and dies. Some say that he struck his head with the hammer and died. Maryam too dies and Khusrav proposes marriage to Shirin. When Shrin finds him in a drunken condition, she curses him for his affair with yet another girl. Khusrav finally return to his palace. Shirin ultimately consents to marry him. Khusrav's son, named Shiroyeh, from his earlier wife, falls in love with Shirin, and considering his father a big hurdle, slays him. He then sends his marriage proposal to Shirin, but before Shiroy could make any headway, Shirin commits suicide and she is buried beside her lover Khusrav. Thus the tale of passions, intrigues, strife and shocks ends.

The Dastan being rife with many dramatic episodes has been very popular with the roaming bards.

The dramatic events, covering as many as twenty years, are roped together by the narration through the art of daastangoi; only the most significant events could be depicted through dramatic action on the stage or through audio-visual media.

There are numerous other long narratives in Kashmiri that have been borrowed from Iran and sing either of the Arab world orIran. The translators have not remained confined to the original text in terms of the backdrop, setting, characters, social conditions, moral values, and cultural elements, but introduced many changes according to their individual choice. As such all the narratives, like Mansoor Nama, Qisa Haroon Rashid, Samnaamah, Wamiq Azra, Sagntarash, Benazir Badar, and many others got easily assimilated into the body of literature in Kashmiri.

There are many narratives that have been borrowed from other Indian languages, particularly, the Punjabi, and Dakni Urdu. Some of these narratives in versified form have remained very popular among the artists of daastangoi.

Gule Bakawali is one of these popular Dastans. The story has been rendered into couplet form by two Kashmiri poets in the early part of the twentieth century, that is Lasa Khan Fida, and N'amatullah Parraay. The two mathnavis, though, entirely different in terms of poetic form, and imagery and diction, have an identical plot that has been borrowed from the Urdu version of Daya Shanker Naseem, a gifted poet of Kashmir who wrote in Urdu. The story of the Dastan is summarised as below: Zain-al Malook, a king of the East, had four sons, but all of them were suffering from one or the other mental handicap, and the king as such was eager to have one more son from his second wife. After many prayers, and performing rituals to propitiate God, he was blessed with the fifth son, but on the condition that he be kept away from the King's sight for eighteen long years, otherwise the omen said that the king would lose his eyesight on having a glimpse of him. Thus he sent away his pregnant wife to a distant health resort where she gave birth to a beautiful prince, named Taj-al Malook. It somehow happens that the king has had a glimpse of the young prince when he was in his early teens. The king eventually becomes blind. The wise Hakim advises him to fetch a rare flower from a distant mountain, and the flower is called Gul-e Bakawul. The four princes set out on a perilous journey to the Bakawul mountain and in their journey are confronted by many mysterious calamities and each time the princes are caught up in one or the other kind of predicament. It is always Taj-al Malook, who in disguise redeems them, but never lets them know that he too is on his mission to fetch the flower of magical healing powers from Bakawal. The most intriguing snare is that of Dilbari Beswa who makes the four reckless princes his slaves and makes them forget all their past by making them taste some magical potion. Again Taj-al Malook's cleverness and sincerity of intent save them from coming out from insomnia. He seduces the guarding ogress of Dilbari Beswa and succeeds in getting information about the location of Bakawul where the healing flower blooms. He goes to the extent of marrying her so that he could bring some relief to his blind father. It the ogress who engages all the rodents at her service to dig out a secret tunnel to the garden of Bakawul so that Taj-al Malook could reach her without being noticed. The wicked brothers again fail him when they secretly steal the flower that he gets from Bakawl.

The unhappy prince Taj-al Malook in his disillusionment leaves in a different direction and founds a new city so that he could gain the attention of his father.

Bakawali somehow comes to know about the disappearance of the magical flower from her garden and sends a letter to Taj-al Malook. The latter, being morally responsible travels to the fairyland of Bakawali and develops physical intimacy with her. Aggrieved by their intimacy, Bakawali's mother Jameela, arranges to send Taj-al Malook to a wilderness where he is held captive by a ferocious giant. With the help of a cousin of Bakawali, Taj-al Malook is freed from the prison and he is married to Bakawali.

Knowing about the secret marriage of Bakawali, who is essentially a fairy, with Taj-al Malook, the king of the fairyland, named Indra is enraged. He changes the form of Bakawali into a stone and keeps it hidden in a temple of a distant island, called Sangladeep. The frenzied lover, Taj-al Malook, uses all his wisdom and ingenuity to know the disappearance of Bakawali, succeeds to reach Sangladeep and on reaching there he demolishes the stone icon and the temple. Bakawali gets rebirth in the house of an oil-seed crusher. And the story ends in the happy marriage of the two.

Thus we see that there are many scenes in the narrative that are suitable for dramatisation through electronic audio-visual media. All the handicaps of de-rationalised scenes and improbability of incidents are overcome by employing various techniques. Here is a dramatised episode of a TV film based on the Dastan of Gule Bakawali:

Scene

The fifth prince, not known to his brothers, enters the front gate of the palace garden. His brothers are seen absorbed in their idiotic activities. The garden and the palace are decorated and illuminated in many colours and designs. The whole ambience is replete with enlivening music to welcome him.

The prince, no more a child, is a sixteen-year-old boy endowed with exceptional beauty. He in his gusto ambles towards the palace of his father.

The four wanton princes are seen enjoying various meaningless gimmicks of the royal fool. They laugh boisterously.

The fifth prince, accompanied by handsome lasses, gradually enters the threshold of the palace. A maid seeing him entering the palace, rushes to inform the royal family. She comes back and stops the prince from advancing further.

Maid: Stop, for God's sake stop there. Do not enter the king's chamber.

Taj-al Malook: You ill –mannered girl! Don't you know that I am the darling prince of the king? Who are you to stop me from entering?

Maid: O mighty prince, you know it well that there is still one day for you to be really sixteen. The Dervesh has strictly admonished us that we should not let you enter the palace until you are sixteen. For God's sake do not advance further.

Taj-al Malook: You mean girl! There is no power that could stop me from seeing my dear father. I have lived full sixteen years in exile and am languishing to see my own father. Get away. (He thrusts aside and walks. The maid cries. On hearing her screams, the king's guards come out and advance angrily towards the prince. Taj-al Malook too blandishes his sword and the guards are scared and keep aside.

One guard: O God, have Mercy, the Prince is adamant to enter the palace.

{On hearing the noise, the king, named Zain-al Malook comes out to see what has happened.}

Zain al Malook: What the hell has befallen you guards? What is this noise all about. Don't you know that this is the time of my siesta after lunch?

A guard: We beg your parden, your Majesty? The prince Taj al-Mallok is obstinate to enter the gate of the palace. We stop him and beseech him to keep away for one day more. This is the decree of the Darvesh.

Taj-al Malook appears before him

Taj-al Malook: O my God. You are great! I finally see my dear father well before me. What a blessed person I am to have my father in front of me!

Zaina al-Mallok, in his uncontrollable fatherly passion moves ahead to hold his prince in his embrace. But all of a sudden he shivers with some strange pain in his eyes.. He holds his face in his two hands. The maids and guards rush to help him.

Zain al-Malook: O God! Have pity on me! My eyes are all embers with heat. I am blinded. I can see nothing. It is all dark around. O God have mercy on this poor servant of yours.!

The four idiot-princes come running and start pushing and imprecating Taj-al Malook for having committed a great sin of blinding his own father.

The scene ends there.

There are many other tales of Indian languages that have been adapted in various *Dastans* in Kashmiri; the *Dastan* of Sohini and Mahiwal is perhaps the most popular among them. The story of the *Dastan* can be summarised like this:

An exceptionally pretty girl, named Sohini, is born to a potter, Tulla of the Punjab. The town in which she was born occurred on the route to Bukhara of Central Asia. Sohini, proved much gifted in embellishing the pots of her father and the pots sold well. She was in her early teens when the trader of Bukhara, happened to visit her village; his name was Izzat Beig. When he chanced to have a glimpse of Sohini at her father's shop, he was immediately charmed by her beauty and her art of decoration. Thus with the excuse of purchasing her pretty pots and cups, he visited the shop almost daily, and finally he took lodging in her house. Sohini, too, fell in love with him. He did all manner of chores in their house and took their buffalos for grazing. He was eventually named Mahiwala, buffalo herder by the local people. When the folks came to know about the love affair of the two, there was resentment among the population. They did not like the idea of marrying a girl of their tribe to an outsider. Sohini's father arranged her marriage to a youth of his own tribe and was sent to the in-laws' house in a doli.

Being unable to bear separation from his love, he renounced the world and decided to live as a Faqir. He took refuge in a hut in the outskirts of the town; the place was not far from Sohini's in-laws's house. When everyone went to sleep, Sohini would visit her lover's hut and spent some time there. She crossed the river by sitting on an inverted baked pitcher and reached the hut. Izzat Beig, caught fish from the river and offered the dish to his regular guest. One day when the river was in high tide, he could not catch any fish. Having nothing to offer to his lover, he cut a piece of flesh from his own thigh and fried it. When she came to know about this, her passion for Mahiwala was more intense.

The secret meetings of the two lovers could no longer remain a secret. One night when she was walking in the dead of night to Mahiwal's hut, she was followed by her cruel sister-in-law. When she knew about the meeting place of the two lovers, she informed her mother-in-law. Sohini's husband was away from the town in connection with some business. The two women therefore decided to kill her. They secretly replaced the pitcher with an identical pitcher, but it was unbaked. When Sohini sitting on the inverted pitcher was in the middle of the river, it dissolved in water. Seeing her drowning in the river, Mahiwal jumped into the river and held his love close to his bosom and thus the two lovers met a tragic death.

The story of Sohini and Mahiwal too has been recited by various *Dastan* singers and has remained as popular as other Iranian or Arab romances. The romance was cast into the form of a *mathnavi* by a gifted *mathnavi* writer of the nineteenth century, named Mohi-ud Din Miskeen.

The *Dastan* of Bul Bakawali has remained very popular and there are several modified versions of the *Dastan* both for the radio and television. Every version has retained the skeleton tale but employed numerous variations in terms of scenes, background sounds, lighting arrangement, series of events, characters, costumes, and the dialogues.

The most popular *Dastan* in Kashmiri has been the *Dastan of Gulrez* originally written in versified form in couplets by Maqbool Shah Kralawari in the second half of the nineteenth century. The story, originally written by Zia Nakhsbi, a poet from South India, is a part of a sequel called 'Totinamah" in which weird birds are seen interacting with human characters and they resolve their difficult problems. The series of Totinamas owes its origin from the seventy tales written in ancient India in Sanskrit. The title of the tales is Shaksaptati, meaning 70 stories narrated by a parrot. The tales were later on translated into Persian by Zia Nakhshabi in 750 AH (=1349 AD). Our gifted Kashmiri poet Maqbool Shah Kralawari read Nakhshabi's summary of the story and rendered it into a long narrative in the *mathnavi* form.

A lovelorn prince, named M'asoom Shah, the darling of his parents, is sitting in his bed chamber and thinking of seeing unseen lands. In the meantime, a weird and highly exotic bird, never seen by anyone before in their land, sits on a bough of a nearby tree. The bird is so charming that the prince grows mad with the desire of having the bird in his cage so that he could entertain himself. All types of seeds are tried to entice the bird, but the bird shows no interest. It is the wise Wazir of the palace who finally reveals that the bird likes only pure pearls as its feed. Eventually, pure pearls ae spread and the bird comes in to feed on them. The bird is ensnared and put in a golden cage. The bird starts talking and beseeches the prince to set it free as it is actually a princess who is under the jinx of her mother for having spent a night with her lover, Ajab Malik, who has been sent to some unknown wilderness. The name of the princess transformed into a bird is Noshlab, daughter of the king of Bait-al Aman, famous by the name of Mashhoor Shah. Noshlab narrates all the adventurous events of her lover, how he was saved in a ship wreck while he was on his voyage to her country to get her. Noshlab also reveals how, Ajab Malik defeated a ferocious giant who had made her sister, Nazmast captive. It was the timely help of Nazmast who arranged for a secret meeting between Ajab Malik and Noshlab. When the two lovers were in deep slumber after their union, her mother saw them in each other's arms and was so enraged that she cursed her own daughter and sent Ajab Malik to a wilderness.

M'asoom Shah, is deeply moved by the pathetic tale of the bird, Noshlab, and promises her that he would brave all dangers, and find out her estranged love. He, carrying the strange bird in the golden cage, left the palace in search of Ajab Malik. After many adventures he succeeds in finding the jinxed lover in a miserable condition. He persuades the parents of Noshlab to allow nuptial relations between the two honest lovers, He succeeds and Noshlab is freed from the curse of her mother. The marriage is consummated with all royal gusto. He himself falls in love with the younger sister of Noshlab and marries her. All leave for their respective homes.

Though the story is quite commonplace in the huge body of literature based on phantasy and imagination, Maqbool Shah ' treatment has made it one of the best classics in the Kashmiri language. There are many dramatic moments in the narrative that could be easily produced for a modern audience through electronic media, like radio and television. Some most dramatic scenes in the series of events are:

CHAPTER 5

Sample Script of a *Dastan* Gulrez by Maqbool Shah Kralawari

Here is a sample of a well written script based on one of the most popular Dastans of Kashmir, viz. Gulrez of Maqbool Shah Kralawari. About the masterpiece Prof. Shafi Shouque writes in his *A History of the Kashmiri Language and Literature*:

> Maqbool Shah did not translate from any particular Persian or Hindustani text of but adopted the plot from the series of tales known under the title *Totinama* (Tales of the Birds) that have been a continuation of a book in Sanskrit, titled *Shaksaptati*, a collection of seventy tales that were an integral part of the folk memory of the subcontinent. Most of the tales are essentially misogynistic in nature as the basic motive of each tale is that the modesty of a woman is always unpredictable and most of the women are infidels to their husbands. A version of *Shaksaptati* was obtained in Persian also and was fairly popular. The tales have a close correspondence with a bunch of tales in Kathasaritasagara of Somannd, and Hatuapdesha. The tales have been translated into several major European languages like German, French, English and Greek. The central character of all the tales is a prince named Madan Sen, and his love Prabhavati. While Madan is away in connection with a business trip, Prabhavati falls in love with the son of the Prime Minister, but it was her pet parrot that engaged her every night in narrating an interesting tale that she could not go to spend a night with the Pime Minister's son. When Madan Sen returned from his errand, Prabhavati tells him that it was their parrot who saved her chastity. Madan Sen and Prabhavati lived a long and happy married life. In 751 AH () Zia Nakhshabi wrote a new version of the tales in highly stylised and rhymed prose. Mughalaq Persian; the text of Zia Nakhshabi's Totinamah was published for the first time in 1910. Maqbool Shah of Kralawor (Budgam District) was inspired by one of the tales of Zia Nakhshabi when he procured an MS of the text and rendered it into a very interesting versified narrative poem, titled Gulrez in 19.... He gives the date of composition of the masterpiece in the following couplet:

Thus we see that Dastans in the past knew no boundaries and easily passed from one culture into another orally as well as in translated texts.

Prof. Shafi Shauq summarises the plot of Maqbool Shah's *mathnavi* in the following words:

A melancholic prince, named M'asum Shah, sitting at the sill of his palace-chamber catches sight of a weird bird, and eventually grows crazy to catch it and have it in his palace. All his attendants try various baits to allure the bird, but fail. It was ultimately the wise minister who suggested that the bird's feed was precious pearls for it was not a normal bird. Thus using the bait of precious pearls, the bird is allured and caught and kept in the cage. The caged bird stops pecking at any pearl and grows emaciated. The prince is very sad and day in and day out thinks of some means to make the bird eat a few pearls. To his surprise the bird moved by the anxiety of the prince all of a sudden starts talking in human speech and narrates its tales of woes to the prince. The bird says that it was actually an unfortunate princess, named Noshlab of a far-off land. She tells M'asum Shah how she was changed into a bird by her angry mother who had seen her sleeping beside her lover, Ajab Malik, a prince of Turkistan, fallen in love with her as he had heard about her beauty through a traveller. The bird (Noshlab) then narrates the story of various adventures of Ajab Malik who, having braved many perils and a ship wreck, had reached an uninhabited island where a jinn, called Afrit, had kept her bosom friend Naz Mast in a grotto. She further tells him how Ajab Malik had fought a battle with Arfit and slain him and released Naz Mast from her captivity and then accompanied her to reach her native land. Naz Mast, in return for her gratitude had promised Ajab Malik to help him find his love, Nosha Lab. It was with the help of Naz Mast that she spent a night in the arms of Ajab Malik in her royal garden. When in the morning, her mother had found her sleeping with a stranger (Ajab Malik) she grew furious and with the use of a curse changed her into a bird and sent Ajab Malik to some unknown desert. Nosh Lab, changed into the pearl-eating bird, tells M'asoom Shah that she had been wandering aimlessly in search of her separated lover. M'asoom Shah, moved by the pathetic tale of the bird, resolves to help the bird-princess, Nosh Lab in finding her lover. Carrying the bird in the cage, he secretly leaves his palace and undertakes a perilous journey in search of Ajab Malik. After many ordeals he succeeds in finding the lovelorn prince Ajab Malik, takes him to Nosh Lab's parents and motivates them to accede to their marriage. Pleased with M'asum Shah's unfailing help, Nosh Lab arranges the marriage of her friend Naz Mast with him. Thus the four lovers, happily live the rest of their lives in bliss.

The tale, though very interesting, is not a linear succession of events, but has many turning points and time-lapses; only a well-constructed narrative could make it interesting. Maqbool Shah, with a thorough mastery in the narrative art has succeeded in this venture and made Gulrez an unparalleled mathnavi in Kashmiri. (A History of Kashmiri Language and Literature.)

Thus it is a challenging task to present the tale in the form of a drama. However, many attempts have been made, but the Qisai Ajab Malik Wa Nosh Lab is unique.

Gulrez

Direction:

The curtain rises revealing the ramp which is lit from both sides, the rest of the stage is in complete darkness.

Musicians playing shahnai and the tune is complemented by melodious drum sounds. They appear at the centre and face the audience. In the meantime light on the stage increases and a group of four girls appear; each carrying a Kangri in her hands. They burn rue seeds in the fire-pots to welcome the musicians with the auspicious smoke.

This is followed by the appearance of a group of Sufi dancers who move in circles as per the style of dance of Derveshes.

One of the dancers comes to the fore and the rest stand in a semi-arc. He informs the audience that the Dastan was written by Maqbool Shah Kralawari in the nineteenth century. He gives some more information about the author and the tale. The narrator thus introduces the importance of the Dastan and also briefly comments on the literary merit and tremendous popularity of the Dastan. Maqbool has adapted the tale of a remote past, about the fourteenth century and given it a local colour. After this brief introduction, he invites the audience to enjoy the same Dastan on the stage.

(A little commotion showing impatience in the hall.)

Bhand: What the hell is making you captive. You could keep all your rags at home, at least for today... Now hurry up. Beat the drums...You suffering from carbuncles...!

The sound of the drums is heard.

The Narrator:

Maqbool Shah wrote at the end of the tale:
khudavandah gunah bahshum mya seeriy
vasielay mya aniy aashaq tsya seeriy

Maqbool, in spite of his achievements, shows his humility and prays for all his sins. We are simply imbibing from his masterpiece to present the story in its dramatic version. We hope this humble attempt of ours is liked by you.

The stage, all of a sudden, is dark as all the lights are switched off. Only the musicians are under the spot light. In the meantime, a spot light makes the king visible, who moves gracefully and stands at the centre of the stage.

The singers sing the following couplets;
The king prayed to God day in and day out,
prayed to the merciful for favour of a son.
He pined to have a beautiful son,
a son pleasing in appearance as well as manners.
Thus his prayers had the desired effect,
God blessed him with an admirable son.

(the first cry of a new-born baby is heard from the background of the stage. A maid comes running:

The Maid: (With her head bowed down)

I pray for the His Majesty's destiny remains always at the zenith, (She sings)

gulaabah phol ze baghi shahi Nakhshab
Sitarah khot zi burji Shahi nakhshab

A fresh rose has bloomed in the garden of Nakhshab;
A brilliant star is born on the horizon of Nakhshab

The King: God is great! O Lord of all worlds! I have no words to express my gratitude. You have saved my kingdom from falling into the hands of enemies. (He takes out necklaces of diamonds and hands it over to the maid. He orders in song:

Let all the treasures be thrown open,
all the needy and the poor should get to their full.

Wazir: The orders shall be abided by, Your Majesty.

With the full orchestra of festivity the stage gradually grows dim. The king retreats.

The dancers start laying down a garden on the stage. Cut braches of all manner are brought, and within a brief time, a semblance of a garden is created.

The lights are turned on, revealing the facade of the palace with huge arches. A few trees are seen behind the palace. The prince enters along with his friends.

One friend: There is hardly anyone in this world to have gained so much knowledge as you.

Friend 2. And who can equal you in other skills? Your knowledge of the unknown too is unparalleled.

Friend 1: You are especially gifted in astrology.

The Prince: I know there is no human being in this world who could be called complete in the realm of knowledge and astrology.

Friend 1: This kind of humility is evidence of your greatness.

Prince: My dear friends, I am an ordinary human being like you.

(In the meantime, a strange bird is seen perching on a tree)

Look there! What a beautiful bird is there in the tree... Oh God! what a beautiful bird. This is really a wonder of nature. I have never seen such a beautiful bird. Really amazing...

The prince moves towards the bird, but the bird is seen flying from one tree to another. The singers sing:

> For its warble the bird was bewitching,
> it bore the plumage that was all shining gold.
> In its colours, its song and visage it was unparalleled,
> With its charms it enthralled all the seeing eyes.
> Once the prince caught sight of the weird bird,
> he too was held in thrall in love for the bird.
> Having caught a glimpse of the bird our prince
> lost interest in music, wine and his comforts.

The Prince: I beseech you O my friends. Find out some means to catch the bird. I must have this bird in my palace. Do something, please.

Friend 1: O your Majesty, it is not easy for us to catch this bird. Whatever we offer it as food, it shows no interest.

Prince: Then what should we do to entice this queer bird?

Friend 2: Our Majesty, forgive us. It is impossible to catch this bird. It is an unusual bird.

Friend:

Be it male or female, every living thin
is created to have food specific to it.
This bird too, might be having its preferred food,
as does a falcon, a thrush, or an eagle.

The Prince: O my well-wishers, my friends, my counsellors. If I fail in having this bird, I shall not live. This crown on my head is meaningless and cannot give any meaning to being. I want this bird.

(While the Prince took the crown off, some pearls fell from it and were scattered on the floor. To their amazement, the bird anon flew near them to peck at the pearls.

Thus they ensnare the bird. The singers sing from behind:

The bird pecked at the precious pearls,
thus they got him easily trapped.
With hunger, the bird started eating the pearls,
it was the greed of its self that got it ensnared.
Greed, indeed, is the burglar of the soul.
Greed, indeed leaves you bereft of thinking.
Once the bird was ensnared for it desire,
the face of the prince blossomed as a garden.

The Prince: My friends, thus we have succeeded in our effort. I decree that the bird should be the centre of attraction for this palace of mine. From now onwards, this bird alone shall be my unfailing friend.

Friends: Our Majesty, then are we reduced to nothing?

The Prince: You are certainly my comrades, but this bird is now my soul, my life. There should never be any scarcity of pearls of its choice.

Friend 1: But our dear Master, that might make the treasure of the palace empty.

The Prince: Why do you worry for that? That is the concern of my father, not you.

Friend 1: The orders shall be carried.

Lights gradually grow dim, leaving a spot light of the bird. Some dancers, wearing black robes, dance round the bird in the cage. The dance is frightening and in the meantime, the prince grows frenzied. All disappear, except the Prince and the bird.

The Prince: O beautiful bird. I cannot bear this plight of yours. Why have you given up eating and drinking and falling sick? If you continue to remain in such a wretched condition, I am sure to die for the worry. Tell me what ails you o bird?

The Bird: I am not mute as you think. (Hearing the bird talking, the Prince is wonder-struck.)Yes I am not a dumb thing. I appreciate how worried you are O Prince. I am really pleased to see you honest and good natured. Had I been in my original form, I would surely seek remedy of your worries.

The Prince: O God! What a wonder you have created. A bird thinking and speaking like a human being.

The Bird (laughing): What could you do if you knew my truth? It is better that you remain ignorant about my plight. That will keep you as well as me happy.

The Prince: But I am bothered about your happiness rather than my own. Tell me if you are a princess, which country do you belong to?

The Bird:

Yes, I am really a princess of a royal family,
but alas a prince, just like you has made me a withered flower.
I never revealed my visage even to the sun,
My father a king is named Mashhoor Shah.

The Prince: If so, what has made you assume the form of a bird?

The Bird: That is a long story O Prince, how can I reveal all to you?

The Prince: But I grow more restless, you see. I want to hear what ails you O princess.

The Bird:

Then be heedful, Noash Lab is my real name,
There is no one other than me to be so unfortunate.
For the last ten long years I have been in this form,
always on my wings, wandering from land to land.
It is not easy to have patience to hear my tale,
I wish, no one else has fallen in love with any other person.

The Prince: Yes tell me what happened to you, tell me all, I am growing out of my patience. Why did you assume a bird's vissage.

The Bird: That is is my tragedy, that is my bad luck.

The Prince: O Noshlab you are a princess. Which country do you belong to? Who is your father? Who is the human being you love so much?

The Bird: There is a kingdom, called Turkistan. The king of the country is very kind and pious, His name is Behzard. He has a son...

The lights are gradually turned off. Singing is heard in the background.

The lights are again turned on, revealing two persons ambling on the fore stage: one old man and the other a young man.

The song:

A youthful man, aloft like a fragrant cypress,
pretty like a pari, graceful, good natured, and energetic.
Brilliant like full moon is his face,
seeing the curls of his hair, the ivy grow envious.
The garden spruce cannot match him in stature,
the one with such a heavenly form was named Ajab Malik.

The Old Man:

Listen O Ajab Malik there in this whole world, in our times
there is a damsel, surely un paralleled in charms and beauty.
There is no other human being so charming as she,
for God has endowed all grace and beauty on her alone.

A silhouette appears on the stage; It is an image of an extremely charming female body.

A song in the solemn voice of an old man in praise of the image goes on in the background.

He is more charming than that of a cypress,
gracefully it ambles in the garden.
Her movement makes the cypresses envy,
Her hanging curls are snares for the deer.
{The silhouette then fades away.}

Ajab Malik:

O revered elder! Inform me
about the whereabouts of the charming fairy in the human form.

The Old Man: It is said that there is a country in the large island. It is a veritable wonderland and is rightly named Bait-al Aman (the abode of peace.)

Ajab Malik: And what about her father and other kin?

The Old Man: I know that her father is a famous king, and she is his only daughter.

Ajab Malik: What is the name of her father?

The Old Man: Mashhoor Shah.

Ajab Malik: O reverend Elder, you kindly help me reach that island. Only then can I have my soul in rest, or I am deprived of all joys of life.

The Old Man: But your father shall not bear the pang of your separation

Ajab Malik:And I, I cannot bear separation from her....... Let me be alone.

{The elder leaves and the lights are put off.}

{The lights are gradually switched on and the stage is lit. Shah Behzard (father of Ajab Malik) is seen conversing with his minister.}

The King: The prince's confinement in his bed, and abdicating communication with all make me think that there must be some cause behind it. You go and explore what ails the prince.

The Minister: His Excellency! I too find myself amazed to see the wretched condition of the prince.

The King: Our royal Hakeem says that there is no remedy of the malady of love... Some elderly person belonging to some unknown land has given the prince the information about the princess of some unknown country. It is the account of the beauty of the princess that has made our beloved prince run crazy.

Minister: Our Majesty. If it is true that our youthful prince is in love with some princess of this world, we shall certainly get her here and present her to the prince. You issue the orders.

The King: O my Minister. I know you are wise and intelligent. You just inquire from people in all corners of our kingdom if anyone knows anything of that princess of the unknown land. I cannot see my dear son suffer any more.

The Minster: Our Majesty. I am myself anxious about our prince. I shall do my best to find the way that he is free from this distress.

The King: I am sure of your prudence that you alone can find the state of his mind. You just go to the Prince as soon as possible.

Use your skill and art to understand him.
Make him express what ails him inwardly.

The Minister: The order shall be abided by. (The Minister exits).

{The king thoughtfully ambles on the stage. The lights are switched off.}

{The lights are switched on. The stage is illuminated again. The Minister reappears. The Prince is seen sitting in a corner with his head drooped.}

The Minister: Enter the chamber. The light is sure to illumine your mind and help you think properly.

The Prince: (Raising his head.) *hah ha hah hah haa*! My thinking? My sickness begins where my thinking stops.

The Minister: (sings from the text)

I have come to know that you have fallen in love with someone,
that is the cause of your sorrow and distress.
Why otherwise could you have saffron-like colour?
Tell me who is the one who makes you so despondent
Tell me clearly who is the one who is your love,
I promise you that we shall get her here soon.
I shall get her even if she is in the sky,
I shall find her out in the remotest corners.

{The prince regains consciousness, gets up and a song is sung in the background.}

Wazir: I have never in my life heard about the king who is famous by the name of Mashhoor Shah.And never has anyone uttered this name Nosh Lab's name unheard to date.

Ajab Malik: Tell me, my Wazir, is the Elder's tale then fiction? Does it mean that Nosh Lab has no existence? Am I then run crazy for nothing? Am I then taken sick without a cause? My wise Wazir, it is no more a thing of humour. This is the time when we have to be serious.

The Minister: O our darling prince. It does not behove a prince to be mad in love for women and renounce the world. And then I might dare to warn you that fidelity has never been true of women; frailty is the essence of women.

Ajab Malik: But you know a lover's love is always fidelity, even if he meets infidelity. This kind of love, once entered the human soul, gives the lesson of faithfulness, besides making one realise the real meaning of life. I am sorry to have to say that you are really ignorant about all this.

Minister: O great prince of the kingdom. I perfectly agree with you. But I am certain that in this known world there is no parallel to your father. He deserves to be called the king of kings.

Ajab Malik: This too is true that there is some great king who is named Mashhor Shah, father of a *huri* – like daughter, named Nosh

Lab. I request you to suggest it to our respected father that he allows me to meet that king. Let us see what destiny has for me.

The Minister: But it is imperative that before you leave to that distant land, we must decide about the people to accompany you.

Ajab Malik: No other than my half-brother, my bosom friend, RasiKh. He alone could make my journey easy.

The Minister: So, then it is decided. I shall in right earnest approach your father. I hope he shall grant permission to the arduous journey...You please be happy. God shall surely resolve all your problems. (The Minister leave...Light grows dim... The king appears under the spot.)

The King: No, never...! How is it possible that our only son, the heir of this vast kingdom, sets out for a journey to a land never visited by any one?

The Minister: But Your Majesty, you know well that his nature is so different. He is never ready to heed anybody's suggestion. He has attained such level in love as lets him not find anyone other than Nosh Lab.

The King: You find some means to make him return from that condition. If he goes that means the end of this kingdom. I shall be ruined.

(Light gradually fades out. A song is heard in the background... The stage is lit again. Ajab Malik accompanied by Rasikh is seen walking on the ramp.}

Song:

From morning to evening they readied for the journey,
Left necessary messages for their other friends.
Early one morning they reached a wilderness,
in quick succession, one wilderness followed the other.
Now on high lands they trudged, then in the plains,
like fast wind they continued their journey.
His friends, for love for their prince, felt wearied,
much tired, yet they journeyed to a distant destination.

Ajab Malik: All my friends are fatigued. Their soles are blistered. O my destiny has involved them too. I repent that I should not have made them accompany me.

Rasikh: Now it is of no avail to think over it...

Ajab Malik:Rasikh, an idea strikes my mind...

Rasikh:What is it?

Ajab Malik: When they are fast sleep in the evening, we shall leave them there and sneak away. They cannot walk further, I know. If any of them gets injured, I shall forgive myself.

Rasikh: But is it wise to run away without letting them know?

Ajab Malik:Why not? All these good friends of mine cannot walk further. It is better, we leave them behind.

Rasikh: But where shall we go to?

Ajab Malik:When they are fast sleep, we shall stealthily go away along with the victuals and money. We shall cross the river, and leave our destiny to God. He alone could show us the path.

Rasikh: Do you mean journey through the river?

Ajab Malik:Absolutely.

(Thunder and lightning)

Song:

In a ferry, they moved away in the river,
They sailed like speedy autumnal wind.
For one full year they had travelled on land,
another year they spent in river-journey.
Finally they found a human dwelling on the bank,
the dwelling was a hamlet of peasants.
They inquired from all about the address of the princess,
But they failed in finding a clue of that beauty.
Her name and address they continued enquiring from all,
no sign they unfortunately found of that beauty.
While both were in deep anxiety, a tempest appeared,
The boat, adrift, was wrecked to pieces.
Their destiny, thus, carried them to the calamity,
the prince, all alone, could barely save his life.
He sailed on a broken slab of the wrecked ship,
on reaching the shore he found himself all alone.

Ajab Malik: O my God! Where am I?...Where is my friend Rasikh?... He alone knew my secrets. He alone was my compassionate friend. For what am I being punished O Almighty? Separated from my parents, separated from all my friends, now I am left hapless and forlorn. Why do you fill my bosom with the ache of love ? Show me some way out, or I might perish in this wilderness. There is no sign of any human habitation.... (Looks keenly in all directions).. Oh, there.. there appears a palace like structure, a strange palace indeed.

(Walks towards the palace and goes in. Lights put out.)

Lights put on again, revealing a fairy sleeping on a couch.

Ajab Malik: O what a strange world is this! Why did the tempest get me here? I lost my companion. I am far away from my parents, I am really helpless... God, save me from this amazement.

(His eyes catch sight of the sleeping beauty and recoils.

Never so charming a pari have I seen,

Is she some angel, or the Moon, or Nosh Lab?

(The pari, awakens, opens her eyes and is amazed to see a human being.)

Pari:

No bird or brute could find a way to this deserted place,
even the lions so mighty shirk for fear.
Impossible that you made your way to this place,
what you are destined to meet here, I do not know.
Was it that you were tired of living your life
that you decided to visit this perilous place?

Ajab Malik: Life and death are decided by God, God alone. You just reveal your story to me.

Tell me about yourself what you are,
A pari, or human being, or a huri or, the moon?
O you bearing the visage of charming pari,
What made you choose this solitary place?

Pari:

Me? Naz Mast is my name, as named by my father,
with much care that respected one brought me up.
One sister, too, I have, named, Mast Naz,
Most thrilled we were when she was born.
I outshone all my friends, in age and charms,
engrossed in carefree pranks we always were.
Precious ornaments and apparel I always wore,
Alas! that Afrit, the demon, appeared anon.
This palace that you see belongs to him,
he is fierce and fearless, and undaunted of all.
For long I have been here all alone confined,
separated from all beings of kind, I am in sloth.
{Ajab Malik, looks around, and evinces fright.}
First you tell me your tale, all the truth,
What made you undertake all the ordeals?

Light gradually fades out. The two are seen under the spot light. The song is heard in the background.

"I hail from Turkistan, a far off land,

I am the prince of that country."

Then he revealed to her own story and of his father,

gave her all the details of address and home.

The Fairy: Nosh Lab? O Prince of Turkistan, our stories are really complicated. It is love that made you leave your kith and kin, and here I am, suffering because of jealousy and hate.

Ajab Malik: I am sure that you shall become a means to attain my destination.

The Fairy: Nosh Lab and I have grown up together; we are bosom friends, inseparable.

Ajab Malik: That is you know Nosh Lab.

The Fairy: I would certainly help you attain your purpose, but alas my destiny is held captive. My body as well as my soul are held captive....I beseech you, you leave this place before the giant comes. You might live longer when out of this place, otherwise he will not spare you.

Ajab Malik: I am already clad in a shroud, and am not scared of death. It is decided that today the giant survives or I... It is my wretched condition that has enfeebled me, otherwise I am strong enough.

The Fairy: It is not a child's play... Think again. I am afraid you might get killed.

Ajab Malik: If you promise to remain beside me, I shall certainly slay that tyrant.

The Fairy: Take hold of this sword, and here is the bow and arrows. Hold God's name in your heart.

{In the meantime thunder is heard.}

Yes, he is come... Be ready now...

{The giant enters.}

The Giant: (Feeling the smell with his nose.)

Who is there in my palace? I smell of some human being here...

Ajab Malik: O stupid being! Why are you so proud of yourself? I shall slay you in a moment.

The Giant: (Thunderously)

ha, ha, ha, ha... You slay me? You?

(He moves left and right on musical notes.)

Ajab Malik: Yes. I am here to kill you. I shall liberate your prisoner and help her reach her home.

The Giant: (Laughing ferociously) You might do so if you survive... Come ahead and combat me... It is alas the last day for you.

Ajab Malik, with his weapons ready, moves forward. He throws just one arrow and the giant falls down prostrate.

The Fairy: Now I am sure God shall certainly fulfil your desire.. You set me free. I do not know how to repay you for all this. I am your attendant from today...

Ajab Malik: God helped us really. The giant is dead and you are free... Thank God who is really great and merciful.

The Fairy: Now we must set out. We must not waste our time. Let us move. Now there is only ambition in my life, that is to help you and Nosh Lab are united.

Ajab Malik: I must send your father a letter. Some messenger shall carry the letter to him... It is a long journey to reach Bahren...

The Fairy:

All right. Let us move faster. I am dying to see my near and dear ones.

Scene

{They leave... The Lights are changed.}

The king is seen holding a letter in his hands. He is followed by his ministers and other nobles.}

The King: O Messenger! You have bestowed new life upon me. Now, I order you my minister, send her my reply, but tell the messenger to deliver it to my daughter as soon as possible. Let him be rewarded in terms of diamonds and pearls.

The Minister: The order shall be abided by.

The King: The whole of our Bahren may be decorated like a bride. All the treasures be kept open! All the poor and needy may be paid to their full.

The commander-in-Chief.

It is really great news that the Ferocious Giant Afrit is slain. It is no less than a miracle.

(Lights fade out... Lights are on again.

There is music of festivity in the background}

Ajab Malik and Naz Mast enter.

The king joyously welcomes them. He hugs his daughter.

The King: O brave young man, called Ajab Malik. You have really proved yourself unmatched brave man...

I do not know how to pay you for the great favour you have done me.

Ajab Malik: Your Majesty, it was possible only when the Almighty wished so. I have hardly any role in this deed.

The King (Laughing): This humility of yours shows that you have the strength of a lion in your body... You made us happy...We shall grant you a respectable position in our kingdom. And we have a special gift for you.

Ajab Malik: Gift!

The King: Yes a gift that you might make you really happy. Your half-brother Rasikh is here.. Let that young man be presented here with honour.

(Rasikh is escorted. The two friends embrace each other.)

Ajab Malik: O my faithful friend do not shed any tears,

Here I am your bosom friend, your heart's solace.

Ajab Malik: Your Majesty! I am really grateful to you for rewarding me thus. I had no hope of his survival.

The King: You should be happy and converse with each other. I shall leave to make arrangements for your stay.

(Lights fade out)

Lights are on again. Ajab Malik and Naz Mast appear.

Ajab Malik: Tell me how long shall I have to stay here? You know, you gave me the promise that you would help me find my love.

Naz Mast: Your long waiting is about to end. Tomorrow she will be here along with her mother.

Ajab Malik: She is my soul. Never seen by my eyes, yet my eyes crave to see her.

Naz Mast: This is what is called Ishq. The mighty love that makes one go crazy, and makes you brave all perils.

Ajab Malik: Tell me how shall we meet? I have no idea.

Naz Mast: You shall stay in my garden. I shall get Nosh Lab to your bower there.

Ajab Malik: I shall be accompanied by my friend Rasikh.

Naz Mast: Why so? You are not afraid of the mighty giant Afrit. Why be so timid in meeting your love?

Ajab Malik: It is very difficult... Not an easy job to meet one's love for the first time.

Naz Mast: No problem. I too shall be there around. The rest you leave to God.

(Naz Mast leaves... Ajab Malik moves about restively)

The stage undergoes a strange change... M'asoom Shah and the strange bird in the cage appear on the stage.

The Bird (Nosh Lab):

A strange message I have received, heed it,

I shall tell you what made me wild with joy.

Nobody knew that good news.

that Nazmast is released from the captivity of Afrit.

(Lights are out....Another spot light shows Naz Mast and Ajab Malik entering.)

Naz Mast: God finally had mercy for me,
that He sent my friend there.
A strange valiant man came there,
he slew that tyrant giant there.
He, thus released me and got me here.

Nosh Lab: But tell me who is this stranger, so bold, so compassionate, and so undaunted? Who is the one who set you free and got you here?

Naz Mast:

A prince he is, mad in your love,
I have given him the promise.

Nosh Lab:

To date no one knows me, and I do not know any one,
Why are you bent to blame me thus?
My life has remained hidden from all to this hour,
no twig of my youth has ever quivered with any wind.

Naz Mast:

He, he from Turkistan has come here in love for you,
He was really crazy in the intensity of love.
Some elderly person had praised your beauty,

that is the secret of his madness in love.
He braved so great a danger and saved me,
I beseech you keep him close to you like a diamond.

Nosh Lab: Where has he gone? Get him here, I would like to see him. I cannot stop myself seeing this crazy man.

Naz Mast: He is waiting, and pining for you in my garden, for the arrow of love has pierced his warm heart.

{The two come forward.. A small tent is opened, Ajab Malik comes out.}

Nosh Lab: O God! Who is the young man so charming? Why has the spear of love struck my innocent heart on the very first glimpse...

(She moves backwards..) Naz Mast is seen whispering something to Ajab Malik. Then he joyously goes near Nosh Lab.}

Ajab Malik: O God! How could the arrow of love strike my heart so soon (He moves aside… Naz Mast whispers to him. And then goes back Nosh Lab).

Ajab Malik:

How can you know how many travailed but for you,
Many an agony I bore in looking for you.
Many a calamity I bore patiently, without a grudge,
The known world I traversed, all dales and mountains.
It is now that my travails finally brought me to success,
I achieved all that my soul languished for.
So long death, grants us freedom to live further,
We together shall live happily never to be separated.
In the earthly world we shall live with a sense of success,
And spend the rest of our life merrily together.

Nosh Lab:

Weird is your idea of having the joy of love with me,
You need to have some human kind as your mate.
You ought to have love with one of your kind,
Never shall you prosper in having love with the other species.
When God produced Eve from the side of Adam,
Adam then enjoyed an amorous relation with her.
Every living being needs to look for the kind of his own,
Never should he have intimacy with one of the other kind.

Ajab Malik:

How many trials I underwent in being faithful to you?
Why are you being so cold and unkind to me?
Now do not dither in letting me fulfil my desire,
Grant me the potion of love and let me be revived.

You, you alone are my life and ambition,
I sacrificed my youth and strength only for you.
Now reveal your visage to my craving eyes,
And see how the dead one is resurrected by you.

Nosh Lab:

You are a human being, while I an elfin,
Do not express what has no foundation.
Vain is your desire to have me as your mate,
Of no avail is your suffering and pain.
Never shall you attain any intimacy with me,
Never shall you be able to douse the flames of desire.
You have better remove the stamp of love from your heart,
That alone shall give you comfort, be wise.

Ajab Malik:

You have really kept your chastity unspoiled,
But my heart is lacerated, my bosom is torn.
Think how I pined for you and withered I am,
Only for you I bore all the pain and suffering,
You, with the hatchet of passion, tore me apart,
Even the roots of my being you did not spear.
Nosh Lab: A human being you are, I am a fairy,
How can our destiny find a way of our union.
You are predestined to be separated, and suffer,
Use your intelligence to seek some remedy.
Be restrained while being intimate with me,
Do not try to go beyond holding me embraced in your arms.
Do not show any lust and spoil my virginity,
Hold your desire as a captive of your control.

{The two come closer to each other, hold each other in an embrace, and lie down.}

Song is sung in the background:

The wine of passion kindled the flames of love,
While keeping a distance they enjoyed the blooms of union.
Goblet after goblet of elixir of love they quaffed,
The two, like Laila and Majnoon thus met in the garden.
When their heads were emptied of reason,
The two garlanded each other's necks in arms.
The unmindful of all they lay in slumber,
Their beauteous faces were glorious in passion.

{In the meantime, Nosh Lab's mother, accompanied by some maids enters. She looks around with searching eyes… She finally finds the two lovers in slumber. Naz Mast silently follows them.}

Mother: Mercy O my God, Mercy! What do my eyes see here? How did my own daughter besmear my honour ?

O Naz Mast, is this the way of gentility?

You got such humiliation to the virtuous.

What made you so hostile to us? And why?

Why did you make my pious daughter so vile in the world?

Did we ever do you any harm? Just prove.

We always held you dear, but why this ungratefulness?

Beware, you shall be punished for this kind of sin,

Always you shall harvest thorns whatever you sow.

But you are not to be blamed, this is my own fault,

I myself mistook onion for saffron.

Naz Mast:

If this is sin, and was caused by me,
forgive me, let your wrinkles from your forehead be gone.

Mother:

I had a very high esteem of you in my heart,
How did I know that our foe, not a friend?
From where did you get this young man, so rash?
Why did you plan to get fire and gunpowder so close?
What land does it hail from, and what is his family?
Whose ill intention made this calamity befall us?

Orders:

Separate the two from each other's arms,
Take care that the secret is not made public.
Handle them in such a way as neither is awakened,
Take care that they should not have any inkling.
You carry Nosh Lab to her bed chamber,
And leave her silently locked up there.
And that crazy fellow should open his eyes in Turkistan,
Or be thrown to hazards in some wilderness.

(In a furious mood she leaves. Light gradually grows dim.}

Nosh Lab, in her bed chamber wakes up, rubs her eyes, stretches, and looks around….Finding her love not there, she grows violent in anxiety. Violent music in the background… Thunder and lightning…

Scene

{Masoom Shah carrying the caged bird is seen under a spot light.}

The Bird (Nosh Lab): And then I ran mad, I lost all manner of senses and distinction. I found neither the garden, no flower, not that friend of mine, nor any sign of him. All those joys and pleasures of yesterday were gone with the winds.

Song: (Sung in a melancholic tone, and accompanied by sarangi notes:

It was morning as heralded by the warble of birds,
I woke up and opened my inebriated eyes.
I knew that I lay on the chest of my love,
It is well said that spring slumber is heavy.
I looked around, seeing neither the garden nor any flower,
Nor did I hear the song of any bulbul.
I saw neither my love, nor that pleasure bower,
Nor was there any sign of the last night's pleasures.
Instead of soothing flowers I saw piercing thorns,
Having longed for a treasure, I met the venomous snake.

Mother: Stop this wailing, stop. Whatever ignominy you had to get me, that you already have got. What for all these laments

Nosh Lab: Mother you, and you alone created the catastrophe. You sent my love away to some unknown place. You should have killed me there and then.

Mother: Yes, there you are true, I sent him to the place from where he had come. That ill-fated rogue.

Nosh Lab: What a disaster you have worked, Oh Mother!

Mother:

You, in our clan, left a scar on your modesty,
You brought shame to our noble dynasty.
I should have celebrated your death,
Your being alive brings me nothing but despondence.

Nosh Lab: But all these tyrannies of yours shall not kill our love, nor shall its intensity diminish. You shall sooner or later be one again. Remember.

Mother: The secret of the misdeed should and now, You should not be able to think like that. See how.

{The mother blows hard at Nosh Lab and she is turned into a bird.)

Fade out… Fade In…

M'asoom Shah with the caged bird. They move about on the ramp. They are seen at a distance.

Song:

Carrying the cage in his hand the prince sets out,
He was accompanied by his trusted friends.
He travelled fast towards Bait-al Aman.
He all alone carried the caged bird on his head.
He thus walked in distant lands, fast as wind.
He called the firmament, merciless powers,
That you made me homeless, and a stranger to myself.
{He is surrounded by goblins and evil spirits, Body theatre is used.}
They held in a circle, and surrounded him,
The unkind forces thus tormented him a lot.
"Which place do you belong to and why come here?
Why you entered this perilous land" they asked him

M'asoom Shah:

I have come from Nosh Lab with good news
A message that dispels gloom and brings joy.
She is in my company, try to understand.
Leave me please, and let me go.
The goblins disperse and let him proceed.

Music..

The mother is seen running towards the foreground.

Mother: O my dearest daughter.. Your separation had turned my heart into a stone.

I cannot bear to see your condition in this cage… I can no more bear the pang…

{The Mother croons some magical words. Nosh Lab returns into her human form.. The two embrace each other.

Mother: See how while alive we got separated,

Nosh Lab: This was writ in our destiny, all was just an excuse.

Mother (to M'asoom Shah):

My son, I had lost my eyesight in her separation,
I wailed all the time and moved about as one mad.
No hope I had to see her again
All hopes of regaining my daughter had vanished.
You made all my agonies vanish, you alone my son,
I shall remain burdened by the heavy gratitude.
A fresh lease of life you bestowed on me,
You brought light to my eyes, Thank you a lot.

Ma;soom Shah: I have but one request, O mother, You are my elder, forgive me if I err.

Mother: Say, say, whatever, you want to say.

M'asoom Shah:

Separation for true lovers is but a doomsday,
Separation for true lovers brings them nothing but death.
I beseech you, be not an obstacle in their re-union.

Mother: Yes I grant you your wish. I promise you.. Send the message to Turkistan.., Request the King of that country to visit Bahren. As soon as possible.

The Narrator enters... Shahnai is played, The Bandh is the Dastan Go

The Bandh: Thus the message was delivered to the father of Ajab Malik. It made him much happy. He was overwhelmed with joy... Yes beat the drum. Yes louder... still louder.. He, followed by his army, thus reached Behrein ... Do you hear me? It was a great and memorable feast... The bride was embellished, She looked like the full moon.

She was decked in her nuptial garments,
All the royal attire she wore, a princess she was.
Loaded she was with precious ornaments and diadems,
He breast too was decked with heavy ornaments,
in rose-pink robes she was clad,
Her body was bathed in the rarest of rare musk

Do you hear me... Ajab Malik advanced and kissed the feet of his father-in-law. Thus the two lovers were in true nuptial bond.

And now think of that good-natured M'asoom Shah.... He fell in love with Naz Mast. And then how could Rasikh be left un-rewarded? She got Mast Naz as his bride. All the three weddings took place simultaneously.. ... I hope you hear me... not one, not two,, three weddings...

All the three young men saw their sleeping destined awake,

From the treasure of beauty each got his share.

The three bulbuls, with three flowers, left that Vale of beauty, or three parrots, won the love of three sweet singing starlings.

Three bridegrooms and three brides appear on the ramp.

Shahnais are played in the background.

A band of Bhands dance ...

The curtain is drawn.

A Voice in the background:

The year was twelve hundred and eighty six,
In mid spring, this narrative was finished.

I had neither knowledge, nor the art of telling,
A vain venture I made in the art of poetry.
The curtain is drawn.. The hall is filled with light.

CHAPTER 6

Conclusion: Art of Staging a *Dastan*

Before we expatiate on how an old *Dastan* could be staged or presented through electronic media, we have to bear in mind that the *Dastan* is essentially an art of the remote past. In order to make it meaningful for the contemporary audience, it has to undergo many changes. The stage is basically a performance area which is meant for the movements of the actors to perform various assigned roles. It has to be quite suitable and adequately equipped to meet the demands of a particular *Dastan.*

The first and foremost condition is that the script has to be prepared on the basis of a *Dastan* according to the possibilities of the present stage and the tastes of the audience. The director and the actors must make a thorough perusal of the script written by a writer who has enough knowledge of dramaturgy. The writer has to write the script in close consultation with the director so that the desired effect is produced.

After a thorough study of the script, the director has to modify the script in collaboration with the writer and then prepare copies of the modified script for individual actors.

The individual actors have also to read the whole script and understand their individual roles. Each actor, representing a character has to highlight his/ her dialogues and stage directions by either underlining the text or using florescent pens. One might write notes about the pronunciation, tune, dialogue delivery, pauses, intonation and accent of all the dialogues in the margins of the text. They have to show their understanding and the directors directions and record them separately, but better in the margins so that they follow each direction and nuance while actual participation in the stage performance. Nothing should be taken for granted, and left for on-the-spot modification. Thus the actors have to perform the function of critical readers who record their impressions. They could also insert their own notes about the setting, cultural background, beliefs, vocations, and nature of various sounds and scenes.

There are many *Dastan* plays that could be presented with a stereo effect by dividing the narrators, or the singers between the two ends of the provided space of the stage. An ideal arrangement is to place Narrators A and B, and C and D at far right, according to the view of the audience.

Experiments in presenting folk stories or *Dastans* on the stage have revealed that the actors performing various roles could be actually shown reading the old texts according to their individual roles. Some very successful arrangements of assigning them position on the stage are as follows:

(i) The readers(actors as well as narrators) are arranged in a row or a semicircle. They may either keep standing or sitting on stools.

(ii) The protagonist or the central characters are assigned a place in the centre.

(iii) The readers(actors as well as narrators) need not memorise the assigned portions of the text, but read the dialogues from the actual paper, held in their hands.

(iv) The music accompanying the portions of the text of a *Dastan* could either be shown physically of the stage or playing in the background of the wings of the stage.

(v) The readers on the stage should not look at each other but straight out towards the audience, or towards some uncertain direction.

(vi) An experiment has been made in devising the exit of a character by simply turning his back to the audience.

(vii) Since the *Dastan* involves the supernatural element, it is not suitable to show scene changes at a very high cost. The changes in time sequence are shown by a group "freeze," followed by some kind of collective shift.

(viii) The director of a *Dastan*-based stage play could use all the paraphernalia and techniques of modern stage craft, like animation, shadows, puppetry, masks, and even computerised graphics in the background. However, it is better to avoid such techniques so that the *Dastan* does not lose its flavour of antiquity.

The director should make the audience make constantly conscious of the fact that they are not watching a piece of reality, but a piece of fiction in the form of art. Art essentially involves artifice and the craft. The more is the distance between actual reality, and the more the characters and settings are de-rationalised, the better is the impact of presenting a *Dastan* on the stage.

We have seen in the preceding sections that the dramaturge of today dealing with the stuff of the past works on the basic principle that in spite of the changes in milieu, social and economic conditions, beliefs, superstitions, and cosmological notion, there are some constant subjects that are universal as well as eternal with the human condition. Some of such themes are:

- Love and passion
- Innocence and experience,
- Infidelity and ungratefulness,
- Incongruities in human nature, and thus humour and satire
- Presence of death and ongoing human strife.

Most of the narratives of the past as well as the present are based on these fundamental conditions of man's existence. Because of the universality of the subjects of all narratives of the past and the present, it is possible to employ the old *Dastan* for contemporary conditions. The art of the *Dastan* cannot be revived in its original form as they are intrinsically rooted in the bygone ages, however, we can successfully use the *Dastan* as a form of technique in dealing with the universal constants, pointed out as above, in the modern context. The whole effort is directed in contextualising a *Dastan*, rather than presenting it in its old form.

Kashmir, the abode of numerous tales of love, ingratitude, exploitation, tyranny, bravery, courage, war, strife, and at the same time a place of confluence of many romances of India and Central Asia, is an ideal place for experimentation in using the narratives of the past in ever-changing contexts. It is an inexhaustible repertoire.

Bibliography

Bhagwat, Durga. *An Outline of Indian Folklore.* Bombay, 1958.

Buhler, G. 1875. *Detailed Report of a Tour in Search of Sanskrit MSS.* Rpt. ed. Shafi Shauq. Srinagar: Jyaykay Books, 2013.

Crook, William. 1895. *The Popular Religion and Folklore of Northern India.* Rpt. New Delhi: Munshiram Manoharlal, 1968.

Dedmar, Khwajah Muhammad Azam. *Waqu'ati Kashmir.* Srinagar: Ghulam Mohammad Noor Muhammad Tajrani Kutub.

Drew, Frederick. *The Northern Barrier of India.* London. 1875 Print.

Dundes, Alan. 1977. *Analytic Essays in Folklore.* (New York: Mouton Publishers.)

Dundes, Alan. 1980. *Interpreting Folklore.* Bloomington: Indiana University Press.

Dundes, Alan. 1965. *The Study of Folklore.* London: Prentice Hall

Dutt, J.C. 1879. *Kings of Kashmir.* (Translation of *Rajatarangani* by Kalhana, Srivara and Jonaraja. 3 vols. Rpt. New Delhi: Low Price Publications, 1990.

Ferrier, J.P. *Caravan Journeys and Wanderings in Persia, Afghanistan, Turkestan and Beluchistan.* London, 1856.

Foucault, Michael, *Technologies of the Self.*

Frazer, James G. *The Golden Bough* (Abridged), London: 1919)

Grierson, G.A. 1932. *A Dictionary of the Kashmiri Language.* Calcutta: Royal Asiatic Society.

Hajini, Mohi-ud Din. *Gaamav manzy phyiry phyiery.* Sonawar: Halqa Adab, 1972.

Hajini, Mohi-ud Din. *Nasirich kitaab.* Sonawar: Halqa Adab, 197O.

Hassan, Shah, 1898. *Taaryikhyi Hassan.* tr. & ed. Shams-ud Din Ahmad, 1989. Srinagar: The Jammu and Kashmir Academy of Art, Culture and Languages, 1989.

Hassan, Shah, 1898. *Taaryikhyi Hassan.* English tr. & ed. Shafi Shauq. Srinagar: The Jammu and Kashmir Academy of Art, Culture and Languages, 2016.

Jarrett, Colonel Henry Sullivan. Trans. *Ain-i-Akbari.* London: 1891

Joseph Campbell. *The Hero with a Thousand Faces.* Bollington Series, XVII, 1949.

Khan, G.M. *Kaeshryan musalmaanan hindy rasm ti rivaaj.* Srinagar: Department of Kashmiri, University of Kashmir, 1979..

Knowles, J. Hinton 1887. *Kashmiri Folk Tales.* London: Kegan Paul, Trench, Trubner, 1893.

Knowles, J.Hinton, 1885. *A Dictionary of Kashmiri Proverbs and Sayings.* (rpt. New Delhi: Cosmo Publications, 2002).

Lang, Andrew. *The Method of Folklore in Customs and Myth.* London: 1884.

Langer, Susanne, *Feeling and Form* (1953).

Lawrence, Walter 1895, *The Valley of Kashmir.* London: Henry Frowde, Oxford University Press. 1895

Leach, Maria. ed. *Standard Dictionary of Folklore, and Legend.* New York. 1949.

Leitner, G.W., 1866. *Dardistan in 1866, 1886& 1893* London: Trubner & Co.

Majid, Gulhan. ed. *Aspects of Folklore with Special Reference to Kashmir.* Srinagar, University of Kashmir.1997.

Miskin, Haji Mohi-ud Din.*Tahaif alabrar fi Zikri al-avliyah'alakhyar, / Tareikhi Kabir.* Srinagar: 1321 AH/1903 AD.

Moorcraft, W. and Trebecck. *Travels in the Himalayan Provinces.* 2 vol. ed. H.H.Wilson. London: 1841.

Naji Munawar, 1981. *Dunyihichi Delyili,* Srinagar: The J&K Academy of Art Culture and Languages.

Naji Munawar, and Shafi Shauq. *keeshir zaban ti adbuk tavaeryikh.*

Srinagar: Ali Mohammad and Sons, 2013

Naji Munawar,and Moti Lal Saqi, 1965. *keeshiry luki baeth.*

Srinagar: The J&K Academy of Art Culture and Languages.

Nazir, Ghulam Nabi, 1978. *Keeshiry depity.* Srinagar: The J&K Academy of Art Culture and Languages.

Nazir, Ghulam Nabi, 1984. *Sanyi gyindan traayi*, Ong, Ww. 1982. *Orality and Literacy: The Technologising of the*

Word. (London: Metheun and Co. Ltd.).

Paksoy, H.B. "*Dastan* Genre in Central Asia" in *Essays on Central Asia.*

Pandit, S.N. *kaeshryan BaTan hindy rasm ti rivaaj*, Srinagar: Department of Kashmiri, University of Kashmir. 1980.

Pandit, SN. *Kashmir Hindu Sanskars.* Jammu: Gemini Computers, 2006.

Pandit, SN. *Kashmir Hindu Heritage, a Study.* Jammu: Gemini Computers, 2012.

Shauq, Shafi, et. al. *Europeans on Kashmir.* Srinagar: Summit, 1997.

Shauq, Shafi. ed. *Hatim's Tales: Kashmiri Stories and Songs* by Aurel Stein, 1910. Srinagar: Gulshan Books, 2005.

Shauq, Shafi. *The Best of Kashmiri Sufi Poetry.* (Mimiographed) Forthcoming.

Shah, Idris. *The Way of the Sufi.* Penguin Books. 1968.

Stein, M.A. 1900. *Chronicles of the Kings of Kashmir,* tr. of *Rajatarangani* of Kalhana. London.

Aurel Stein, 1917. *Hatim's Tales: Kashmiri Songs and Stories* Rpt. ed. Shafi Shauq, Srinagar: Gulshan Books, 2005. pp.4-12.

Sufi, Ghulam Mohi-ud Din. *Kashir.* 2 vols. Lahore: Punjab University, 1949.

Teng, Mohammad Yousf. ed. *Sheerazah, Saqaafat* number. Srinagar: The J&K Academy of Art Culture and Languages, 1966.

Teng, Mohammad Yousf. *Talaash.* Srinagar: Author, 1988.

Ved Kumari, Dr. *The Nilamata Purana,* 2 vols. Srinagar: The J&K Academy of Art, Culture and Languages, 1968.

Vigne, G.T.1842. *Travels in Kashmir, Ladakh, and Iskardu.* 2 vols. London: Henry Collburn.